He Kept Me

See Yourself on the Other Side of Through

Tanya Dickens

He Kept Me

See Yourself on the Other Side of Through

Tanya Dickens

Designed by: Tayla Dickens
Illustrated by: Taya Dickens
Edited by: ShanLan

ISBN 9780692816790

Contents

Preface

I wrote this book to encourage you to trust in the Lord with all your heart and do not lean on your own understanding. The references in this book were taken from the King James Version of the Holy Bible unless noted otherwise. **When writing this book and through my life experiences, I have learned to trust in these affirmations:**

- The Bible says we overcome by our testimony and the blood of the Lamb.
- Know that with God all things are possible, if you believe.
- Believe that there is hope for the hopeless, so don't give up.
- Fear and revere the Lord knowing that no matter what you are going through, God is able to do above and beyond all that you can imagine. Now, imagine yourself on the other side of through.
- Eat the meat and throw the bones away, meaning we will have trials but in every one of them, there is something for which to be thankful. Give thanks, learn and/or discard the rest.

God has always smiled on me. I thank Him for His grace, mercy and favor. I thank God because He kept me.

Acknowledgments

First, I give honor to my Lord and Savior, Jesus Christ. I thank God that not only do I not LOOK like what I have been through, I no longer FEEL like it.

I am so blessed and thankful for:

- My husband Stevie (Steve) for his love, support and prayers.
- My fearless son Timothy, for his strength, courage, love and support. Writing this book would have been extremely difficult to accomplish without those things. I dedicate Regina Belle's song "If I Could" to him.
- My beautiful daughters Tayla & Taya who cheered me on every step of the way! They said, "Mom you have to do it, you have to tell of the wondrous works of God and how He kept you."
- My loving and supportive mother, the most genuine and upstanding woman I have ever known.
- My amazing father (stepfather) for his unconditional love, support and guidance.
- My incredible siblings for loving and supporting me always.
- My wonderful Pastor and First Lady for not only teaching God's Word but being doers of His Word. I am also thankful for their transparency and for sowing into my life daily. I also give a special thanks to my former Bishop and his wife for the foundation I received from them.

1

Introduction

In November 2009, I typed a letter about the miracle that God had performed on my son, Timothy. I made 250 copies and my husband put a copy in every mailbox in our neighborhood. It was important for me to distribute those letters because in the midst of the storm, I told God "When He restores sight to my son's eyes and hearing to my son's left ear, I would tell it everywhere I go" and that's what I've been doing. People need to know that God is still in the miracle-working business. He is the same God He was yesterday, this day and forevermore. Everything that He has done in the past, He can and will do it now. I am a living witness that **ALL** things are possible, if we just believe.

The letter stated:

> Hello,
>
> My name is Tanya and I am a Lakeview resident. I am writing this letter to share 2 of many awesome testimonies with you.
>
> My son was born with Sickle Cell Disease (SS) a chronic blood disorder. He has had many pain crises, hospitalizations, blood transfusions, seizures, strokes, necrosis of the bone and other health issues as a result of this terrible disease. We have been praying 22 years for healing and a cure for this sickness.
>
> In 2007, my son started losing his vision. Then he lost his vision in both eyes and hearing in his left ear. I took him to seven hospitals, including Washington Hospital Center and Georgetown University Hospital. No one could help. The doctors ran all kinds of test, they brought in the stroke team, the neuro-ophthalmologist and no one could help. I was told there was nothing they could do; he was

permanently blind. It was very rough on us. Not only did he have severe pain crises and hospitalizations but he was blind and could not hear in his left ear.

We prayed and prayed and asked God to perform a miracle as we had read about in the Bible. My son grew tired of his situation and began to give up. He said, "I no longer want to live, after all, what do I have to live for?". He said, "I'm in severe pain everyday…all day. I am taking pain meds around the clock (still did not take the pain away) and now I can't see or hear in my left ear." I told him that I don't believe that this is his story… to live with sickness and pain all of his life and to die. I just refused to believe that.

On May 4, 2008, around 4 a.m., I prayed with my son for several hours. I felt God's presence and I told him if he would just call on Jesus, just as sure as I was standing there that He would restore his vision and hearing. My son called on Jesus but not really believing. He said he didn't want to hear what I was telling him because if it could happen, then why hadn't it already happened? He also said I didn't understand what he was going through. He was absolutely right. So, I had to talk to him at his level, where he could better understand.

I told him that I know he likes Lil Wayne. If he was at a concert and Lil Wayne asked "who wants the bling bling" he'd be yelling his name because he wants what he has… well that's how he needed to call on Jesus because He was there and He had what he needed. He still would not call on Jesus.

We went to church and had a great service. When it was offering time, I told my son to sit there and I'll be right back because I'm going to put in my offering. As I got to the front of the church, a woman stopped me and asked about my son. I told her, he's doing great and she asked, "Oh can he now see and hear? I responded, "No, but God got it all under control." She said, "I'm sorry…you just look so happy, so I thought he was okay." I told her, "Well I ain't trying to look like my situation because I would be a hot mess and I said but yes he's okay and let me get back to him because I don't like leaving him for very long.

As I was walking up the aisle watching him, it looked like his eyes were following me. When I got closer, I said, "It looks like you can see me!" He waved his fingers at me and said, "I can see you!" God restored my son's vision and hearing at that moment! Glory be to God!

Now at the beginning of the letter I stated that we had been praying for healing and a cure for the disease, called sickle cell, that my son was born with. On August 7, 2009, my son had a bone marrow transplant and I was his donor (glory be to God). This transplant cured the sickle cell. I received a call and was told that my son had taken on my DNA and that no sickle cells were present. Thank you, Jesus!

I know this was kind of lengthy, but I told God in the midst of my son's blindness and deaf ear, when He restores his vision and hearing, I would tell it everywhere I go! And that's what I do! Thank you for reading and I pray that if you are going through anything in your life that our testimony can/will give you Faith to keep on keeping on.

2

My Son

I thank God for my son, my first born. Shortly after birth, I was told he had sickle cell anemia with hemoglobin "SS", the most severe form of the chronic blood disorder. The disease itself can cause severe pain and permanent damage to the heart, brain and other organs. I have heard some describe the pain from sickle cell as feeling like someone was stabbing them with a butcher knife…repeatedly. There were times that I could not touch his body where he felt pain because my touch was too painful to bear.

My son suffered many years because of the sickness and we spent an innumerable amount of days and nights in the hospital because of it. As stated previously, my son suffered most of his life in unimaginable pain as well as dealing with other health issues because of the disease. I remember when he was only a couple of months old and would cry inconsolably with swollen hands and feet. Then, my father would take us to Children's Hospital. The swelling was a sign of a pain crisis when he was a baby. As he grew older, the symptoms changed, and the pain crises worsened.

My son was unable to attend school regularly and he was unable to participate in a lot of activities because of his illness. Not only did he miss out on the physical activities but also his social development. This was tough for him to deal with because he was just a kid living with a life-threatening disease.

Raising my son with sickle cell disease also took its toll on our livelihood and finances. Most of the time, I was on leave without pay (LWOP) and other times I was absent without leave (AWOL) or on leave restriction. I always thanked God, however, that I had a job that provided us with health insurance.

I learned about God's Word and how to pray to Him at a very young age. One thing that stood out to me back then was the scripture in the Bible (Matthew 9:20-22) regarding the woman with the issue of blood and how God healed her. Knowing that God is not a respecter of persons, He loves me just as He loved her, so I believed He could and would heal my son of the blood disease he had. Then I would remember a song about someone touching the hem of His garment and being made whole, not realizing the two were one in the same. I remembered those things and I prayed often, asking and expecting God to heal my son.

My son still suffered and sometimes it seemed like he was getting worse. I wondered if God had heard me. Then, I started thinking that maybe we're supposed to touch the hem of the bishop's robe to get the healing because God is a spirit. So, where was this garment and how were we supposed to touch it? I knew that God was real, and I believed His Word was true.

One thing I didn't know and could not understand was why my son had to suffer the way that he did. After all, he was a child and he didn't ask to come here. Why so much pain, I asked the Lord many times. As I began to read my Bible more, I realized that there were many who were afflicted, and God healed them. I just needed to wait on the Lord and be of good courage…even when I didn't feel like it.

I remember in July 1995; my son was in the hospital and he was having one of the most painful crises I had ever seen him experience. As a matter of fact, that hospitalization lasted no less than 20 days. The thing about sickle cell disease was that the pain crises would happen out of nowhere and the length of time each crisis lasted varied. My son was in severe pain. The nurses were having a difficult time starting an IV line without blowing his veins and most of them had pretty much been used.

One day around noon, a doctor came in to talk with me about the fluid that was found around my son's lungs. The doctor told me that surgery was necessary and that I needed to sign some papers. I read them, and I remember reading if something were to happen to him, perhaps death, that the hospital would not be held responsible. I was scared so I called my mother. She was away from her desk, so I put the papers on the table. Shortly thereafter, a different nurse came in, gave him an IV, administered some morphine for pain and he had finally fallen off to sleep.

Not even 15 minutes later, my son started talking in his sleep about my younger sister teasing him and of course she wasn't there it was just he and I in the room. I pretty much ignored him as he appeared to be hallucinating. Minutes after that, my son's head lifted slowly off the bed, and he said to me, "Tanya, I'm going on to the other side" and I said okay, thinking it was the morphine causing him to talk out of his head. Come to find out, it was like he was letting me know he was leaving me.

Suddenly, the monitors that were connected to his body started sounding loudly. There was a lot of beeping and the numbers on the monitor were dropping. I shook him and called his name before opening the door, screaming and yelling for help! The nurses and doctors ran in, they lifted his body and it was limp. He was not responding.

One of the nurses told me to sign the paper that I had been waiting to discuss with my mother. I signed it as they rushed him down the hall to surgery. I was told that my son's lungs collapsed, and he was suffocating in his sleep. I prayed and asked God to please let him live as I felt so bad for giving him the okay to go on to the other side.

Then, there was a time my son started to lose his vision. First, it happened to one eye and shortly thereafter, the other. His hearing in his left ear was also lost at that time. There are no words to explain what I was feeling for him and what I was feeling, myself, as his mother as I watched him try and make it each and every day.

Before he lost his vision, we would watch television together. After he lost his vision, I remember I turned on one of his favorites, "Martin", as we sat on the sofa in hopes that he would say he could see, but he didn't. Then, I would leave on the light in his room all day and all night along with the television but without the volume, hoping for the day I would hear him say, "Dang, it's all bright in here…" but that never happened.

Losing his vision and hearing did not stop the sickle cell pain crises and other health issues that went along with it from happening. There were many days and nights I spent in the emergency room with him until the wee hours of the morning, not wanting to leave him there alone. Unfortunately, I had to work and one of my daughters had school.

Thinking back to one time in particular, my daughters and I were at the hospital with him until close to midnight; all three of us were tired and sleepy. I remember putting two chairs together against the wall, laying the girls across them so they could rest, and I sat on the floor so if one had rolled off they would roll onto me.

Then, there were those times I would find my son laid out in the floor because he would fall out, out of nowhere with no warning. I remember going out to run errands and he was babysitting his younger sisters. When I left out, my daughters were in the basement playing and he was in his room listening out for them.

When I returned, I called out to him to help me bring in the bags, he didn't answer. The girls were still playing in the basement, but they said he was not down there. I ran upstairs frantic that something had happened to him and he wasn't there either. I then proceeded back down the stairs and into the basement where I found him lying in the stairwell unresponsive. I called 911 and they came. It was terrifying! We later found out that my son had a subdural hematoma which ended up correcting itself without surgery. Glory be to God!

A few years ago, my son had a right hip core decompression and a total left hip replacement because he had avascular necrosis, another complication resulting from sickle cell disease. Thank God it was a successful surgery.

As if the pain and suffering associated with sickle cell disease weren't enough, there was the time he was dumped outside in the cold as if he were garbage.

It was a cold Sunday morning. I received a call from a woman at Doctors Community Hospital telling me that my son was dumped on a bench outside of the emergency room.

We had just gotten out of church and rushed right over. When we arrived, there laid my son on a bench in severe pain. He was in so much pain that he could not move his body at all.

My daughters and I tried unsuccessfully to lift him; he was much too heavy. Not to mention, every touch caused him more pain.

I was angry and hurt! They had to have known dumping him outside in the cold would cause him to have worse pain.

Feeling helpless, I went inside practically begging for assistance. My son was again seen by a triage nurse then immediately taken in the back to have an I.V. and pain medication administered.

I spoke to the doctor that discharged my son. He was very rude as he told me that my son was well enough to go home; that his bloodwork "looked good." Then he told me that our health insurance was not accepted at Doctor's Community Hospital and that the hospital was for sick people.

Holding back my tears, I told the doctor that my son was sick and in excruciating pain as he could clearly see. Then I explained to him that the paramedics will take him to the nearest hospital; they don't ask about health insurance.

I told him all that he had to do was start treatment then contact our health insurance company to have him transferred.

Instead of hearing me out, he then warned me that the same thing would happen if my son comes there again and he's not either bleeding or dying.

My son was transferred to a different hospital where he was admitted for a pain crisis. He also received a blood transfusion because his blood counts were very low, contrary to what the doctor told me.

God has healed my son time and time again. I will continue to trust and believe in Him for the complete healing of my son's body despite being told that sickled cells were found in his blood again.

3

My Foundation

Many have asked me how I developed the faith that I have and how I learned to trust God the way that I do. My simple answer is experience; experience is my teacher.

I grew up spending many days and nights at my grandparent's house. My grandmother was an amazing woman and if I had to describe her, I would describe her as a praying woman. She was so full of love and kindness. I learned through her how to love and forgive those who spitefully used me.

My grandmother raised her family of 17 children and never missed a beat at being a beautiful and honorable wife to her husband, my grandfather. Grandma gave unselfishly of herself to everyone. I thank God for her.

I thank God for allowing my grandfather, a reverend, to preach and teach me the Word of God because without that foundation, I don't know where I would be or in what condition. Putting God first in all I do is something I thank God for allowing my mother and my grandparents to teach me.

I also thank and praise God for my mother: "Mama", is what I call her. She always took great care of us. She loved us and was very protective over us. Mama was not a woman to hang out; she spent most of her time with us when she was not working. She taught and instilled in me to treat others how I would want to be treated.

I admire my mother's character. Mama says what she means, and she does not straddle the fence. She has never been a people-pleaser. My mother is known by many and I can honestly say that I've never heard anyone speak ill of her.

Mama had four children. I am second to the oldest. My big brother is one year older than me and twin siblings, nine years younger. My big brother and I have the same biological father, who died when I was around two years old.

I don't remember anything about my biological father other than what he looked like and that's only because of pictures. Some of my aunts told me that I look just like him and that he loved me so much. It's too bad I have no recollection of him. It's also too bad that I never had a relationship with his side of the family despite running into my paternal grandmother several times as a child and giving her our contact information. I would have loved for my paternal grandparents to have shared stories about my biological father and some family history.

I would be remiss if I didn't mention my Uncle Randolph and Aunt Fannie who told me to meditate on scripture, Isaiah 53:5, which reads: "But he was wounded for our transgressions, he was bruised for our iniquities; the chastisement of our peace was upon him and with his stripes, we are healed." I was 16 years old when they taught me that scripture and I can honestly say it has sustained me for many years.

4

Growing Up

Up until around the age of 13, we, my big brother and four-year-old twin siblings, spent a lot of time at our maternal grandparent's house because our mother had to work. Unfortunately, we never had any contact or communication with our biological father's side of the family.

Spending time at my grandparent's house was so much fun. There was always a lot of people there as we had a very large family. As I mentioned earlier, my grandmother had 17 children and some of them had children as well, which made it lots of fun.

We would be outside running, jumping, playing jump rope, playing tag, swinging on the tire that hung from a tree and as we got older, we would play football in the street. We would also have dance contests, which I won most of the time because I was the best dancer. Some of my uncles would build go-karts out of wood for us to ride; boy that was some fun! They learned to build a lot of things from my grandfather. He could build just about anything.

As a matter of fact, we would often help him out by carrying wood and cinder blocks from the front yard to the back yard, where he would be working. Speaking of working, I remember when we, my big brother and our cousins, would go around the neighborhood with our plastic bags, collecting aluminum cans and my grandfather would take us to the store to recycle them for money. If we weren't outside we would be inside playing with the race track, the electric football game or Vectrex, a video game. Of course, there was plenty of fights and name-calling among the grandchildren which wasn't unusual.

One thing about those fights…they wouldn't last long. We would be right back outside playing together. There was never a dull moment at my grandparent's house. Even though there were a lot of us grandchildren, there were also enough of my aunts and uncles at home to help look after us.

My grandmother could be found sewing, cooking and minding the home for the most part. Grandma sure could cook! I always looked forward to going there after school. As soon as I'd walk through the door, I could smell the aroma of something delicious coming from the kitchen.

Grandma had a heart of gold! I remember when she would sing songs about "the windows of heaven being open" and "praying right through because God knows, and He understands, He knows just what to do, don't be discouraged, pray right through." Grandma would tell me that God is a friend to the friendless and He will stick closer than a brother. She would also tell me weeping may endure for a night, but joy will come in the morning.

I remember her saying those words to me as if it were yesterday. I thank God for my grandmother and the strength, courage and faith she has shown and taught me throughout my life.

Another thing about visiting my grandparents' house, we had to get up very early in the mornings and come together for church services. My grandfather was a reverend and we would pray, read the Bible, sing and give testimonies. This was every day, not just on Sundays. There would also be church services at the house on some evenings. Those services would also consist of praying, reading our Bibles, singing, giving testimonies, paying tithes and offerings to my grandfather.

I remember my grandfather would always tell us to be like a tree, planted by the water and to pray without ceasing. We would also spend a lot of time tarrying. Tarrying is when we would call on Jesus for what seemed to be a long time. I remember I would lift my head a little and peep to see just what was going on. Oftentimes, I would catch the eye of someone else who was also peeping as well.

I had no idea all that praying, fasting and tarrying would be the foundation that I needed for the things to come later in my life.

5

Seen but Unseen

As a child, I grew up with what I call the "you better not!" and "don't let me find out!" syndrome. In my mind that just about cut off all communication. I witnessed a lot of things from drug use to sexual abuse. One time, I saw the sexual abuse happening and the person committing the act saw me, I got the worst look I had ever seen and was told to get in the room and that I had better not say anything, or I would get it. Get what, one might ask but I knew "get it" meant get my tail whooped! Needless to say, I never told anyone.

Apparently, I wasn't the only one who saw or knew about the sexual abuse because I had heard others talk about it. I would let the other children speak on it first and even then, I was hesitant about saying anything. Lord knows, I didn't want anyone saying I told them about it. Witnessing such abuse was way too much for my young eyes to see.

I'd even heard the grownups talking about sexual abuse within my family mostly bits and pieces, never in its entirety. As I got older and heard more talk about sexual abuse and asked questions, it was always swept under the rug meaning no one talked about it. Whenever I brought it up, it was always "I don't want to talk about that stuff" or "so and so is very nasty," and "don't go around him" but never with any explanation.

It seemed like, sexual abuse was ok but not ok. It seemed like it was normal because everyone went about the day as if nothing ever happened. Another reason I said it seemed like it was normal is because no one went to jail, those who knew about the abuse acted as if it was just one of those things that happened, but no one ever talked about it. Everyone seemed to get along.

As I got older and went through the things I have gone through, I told myself, the buck stops with me. I would be transparent with my children and I would let them know that there is no question that they had that would go unanswered. I have come to realize that history has a way of repeating itself if a thing is not exposed and dealt with. I decided that my children would have a normal life and that my issues would not be passed on to them.

By the time I was 14, my mother would allow my big brother and I to stay at home alone and babysit our younger siblings. My big brother was cool; hanging out with him was a lot of fun but sometimes we would get into arguments and push one another around.

Mostly we would just call each other names though. My big brother's favorite name to call me was tomboy. I remember the day he upgraded me to a super tomboy. We were just doing what siblings did, made fun of one another, not really meaning any harm.

As for school, it felt as if I was present at school but not present in school because sometimes I didn't remember being there. I was bullied a lot. I didn't feel pretty, and I had low self-esteem. My grades were average in middle and high school, however, I failed physical education miserably because I would not change into my uniform. Most people would say, that's the easiest "A" one could earn but not in my case.

My big brother was a popular dude all through middle and high school. Many people didn't even know we were siblings. I'm thinking that had a lot to do with us being totally opposite; he was outgoing, and I was "going out" of my mind.

He had no idea I was going through so much because if he did he would have protected me as usual.

My big brother also had no idea that I was very angry with him; it was probably more like jealousy though. I should not have been angry with him but that's how I felt at the time. I mentioned earlier that my mother had twins, a boy and a girl. I was angry at him because he didn't seem to have any responsibilities.

He could go outside and play whenever he wanted. He could visit our grandparent's house and spend the night, again, whenever he wanted. My big brother seemed to have been enjoying life and having fun.

Me, on the other hand, was responsible for babysitting both of my younger siblings. I could no longer spend the night at our grandparent's house because I had to stay home and help with my siblings and that made me angry. I can recall one time in particular my mother telling me I could go and spend the night at my grandparent's house and I got so excited. My younger brother started crying because he did not want me to go and my mother then changed her mind and said I couldn't go. There were no words to describe what I felt.

I was mad, sad and crying. I went into the bathroom and sat there until I got myself together. As soon as I walked out of the bathroom, my big brother was there to make things worse by smiling and teasing me about not being able to go. This was not the first time and it certainly wasn't the last time. My big brother would tease me regularly which would really upset me.

It wasn't that I didn't want to help babysit my siblings, I didn't feel that it should have been my responsibility most of the time. I thought that my big brother would be responsible for my younger brother and I would be responsible for my younger sister. That didn't happen, I was responsible for both and I resented it.

6

New Family

One day, my big brother came home and said, “Guess what? We have three brothers” and with excitement I asked, “Really?! How? How do you know? How old are they?” My big brother answered me saying “our biological father had three other sons and their ages are like 20, 19, and 18.” He told me that he had met our uncle, our deceased father’s brother, and that he had told him all about them. I was super-excited!

The following week, my big brother came home again talking about them and I asked when we could meet them, and he said he already had. I remember thinking, “here we go again, he doesn’t have to come straight home from school, he could hang out and didn’t have any responsibilities.”

He said he had met our biological father’s oldest son. I wanted to know when I could meet them, and he said soon and that our biological father’s oldest son wanted to meet me as well. My first thought was, “Yay! Finally, I’m going to have other brothers who will get my big brother for always teasing and making fun of me! They’re going to defend me, and I am going to be alright!”

My next thought was “I’m their only sister and they are going to love me and take great care of me. They have jobs and they will buy me pretty clothes so that I’ll fit in at school!” I was hoping they would share pictures of our biological father with me. I was also hoping they would tell me how our biological father felt about me. Our day to meet had finally come!

My family and I met my biological father's oldest son at a local skating rink. I am not sure why his other sons did not come. We met and with excitement I said, "wow, you look just like our father!" Although I had not remembered my biological father, I did however, remember his photos.

We hugged, and he was just as excited to meet us. Later that afternoon, I can recall my mother saying to us, "Uh huh, it's okay that y'all met and everything, but don't get mixed up with them because I've heard a lot of stuff about them boys. They were bad, and they got into a lot of stuff." I asked, "Mama, what are you talking about? He seems nice." She said, "just like I said, them boys got into a lot of stuff…they stayed in trouble." That went in one ear and out the other.

After the initial meeting, my biological father's oldest son started hanging out more often with my big brother. He eventually brought his son over to meet us. I was excited to become an aunt. Next thing you know, my biological father's oldest son would come to our house to hang out regularly and we had cash fun! He was a jokester and would have us laughing all the time.

Meanwhile, my mother would still be saying, "I done told y'all, y'all don't listen, y'all are being hard-headed." I would be thinking, "Dang, Mama always thinking something bad going to happen." My big brother and I went to our biological father's oldest son's house where he lived with his mother and younger brothers. We met them and one of our brothers had the exact same name as my big brother. I wondered how they did that; how can they have the exact same names?

The meeting went well, and everyone was happy (especially me) to have met our other family. Now, I knew I would be able to get out of the house sometimes. Those days of feeling jealous of my big brother because it seemed like he could come and go as he pleased were about to come to an end.

Our biological father's oldest son invited us out and my mother said I couldn't go but my big brother could. I remember him saying "Dang, your mother doesn't let you do anything." I said, "Yea, I know, and it gets on my nerves!" It seemed that he understood my misery.

One day, he taught me how to catch the bus to their house because I loved to hang out over there. Actually, I wanted to hang out anywhere other than at home all the time. My older brothers and I would be outside, and they knew everyone; they were well known. I met a few of their friends, some girls and some guys. Sometimes, we would be outside and their buddies from around the way would try to talk to me and get my telephone number and they would quickly shut them down. They would let them know that I'm their only sister and that I was only 14 years old.

I remember hanging out at their house listening to their mother talk about them and the things they had done. Sometimes, I would overhear bad things too. I overheard talk about criminal activities, for which they did time in jail. I started thinking about what my mother had told us.

After visiting more often, I met my biological father's oldest son's girlfriend; she was fly. She seemed very nice, she was pretty, her hair was beautiful, and she dressed very well. I liked her and was so pleased to meet her as I thought she could take me under her wing and make me fly and I'd be the cool girl at school. I felt that things were starting to look up until…

One day, my biological father's oldest son called and said he had a present for me and that if he saw my big brother he would send it to me by him. That didn't happen right away so one day being so excited about what it could be I called my mother to ask if he could bring it to our house. I had to call because Mama didn't allow us to open that door for nobody! She hesitated at first, but then she said I could and told me to lock the door and call her as soon as he left. By now, Mama had a chance to see that "those boys" weren't as bad as she thought.

I called and told him he could bring my present to the house. He came over and he asked if my step-father was home and I told him no. So, I opened the bag and it was 2 Adidas sweat suits inside, a pink one and a red one. I was super happy! I had always loved Adidas but never had any Adidas clothing.

He asked me to try them on and he said let me see how you look in them. As I started to walk into the back where my room was, he said try it on out here. Looking away with a puzzled face, I thought to myself, "that's strange" and feeling kind of awkward I told him, "I don't change in front of boys." He told me that he's my brother. I said, "Ok, but I don't change in front of my other brothers either." I went into the back and as I was changing, I began to feel weird and kind of uncomfortable. I came out and showed him.

He said ok, try the other one on. I was already uncomfortable at the mere thought of him asking me to change in front of him the first time, so I said to him, "Well they're the same size, so I really don't need to try it on." He told me to try it on right there, not in the room. I was threatened, choked and sexually abused. Guess what? He also told me the same thing I had heard so many times growing up, "You better not say anything," so I didn't.

That day changed my whole life.

I became very distrustful of people, angrier than I had ever been. Whenever someone did something nice for me or gave me anything, I always felt like they wanted something in return. After all, no one will just "give" me anything and no one is just a "nice" person. I didn't have many friends already and it was going to stay that way.

My biological father's oldest son still came to visit and hang out with us many times after that and we would still go and visit their house. For the most part, all was well and while I tried to make myself believe that I could see and treat him as my brother again, what he did would always remain in the back of my mind.

Most times, it was just another day with the brothers and it was fun hanging out with them. I remember there was time when I was visiting, and his mother left to go somewhere, then it was me and two of my biological father's oldest sons. One of them ended up saying he was leaving. Not wanting to be left there alone with the abuser, I asked him if I could go with him and he said, "Naw Tanya, you can't go where I'm going" and I remember asking him why not and he said, "Because you can't." Then I asked him not to go and he said he'd be back. After he left, I was abused.

Most of the time my biological father's oldest son acted normal like he did in the beginning before the abuse started.

One day, he invited me to go to Wilmer's Park to see a few Go-Go bands play live with his then girlfriend, who he later married. I rode in the car with her and her friend. I sat in the seat directly behind her. I wanted to reach up and tell her what had happened to me. However, after listening to her talk to her girlfriend about him and some things they were going through, I thought to myself, she can't even help herself, she surely can't help me.

I felt that she would tell him what I said and he in turn would do something to harm me like he so often told me he would. So, I continued to not say anything.

7

The Truth Will Make Me Free

One day while sitting in school, I remember daydreaming as I had done so many times. Some people would think I was staring at them and would ask me why I was staring while others would say they wish I would stop staring at them. I wasn't though. I was in deep thought about all I was going through.

My mind could not contain all that had happened to me. Here I am trying to learn but I am constantly thinking about the abuse or his words that he would kill me if I told on him. There were times I couldn't even remember daily activities from all the stress. To top that off, I wasn't sleeping well because I started having nightmares about what was happening to me…or so I thought.

Meanwhile, my menstrual cycle was late. I was thinking, Lord, please don't let this mean I'm pregnant. I remember telling my biological father's oldest son that I was going to tell on him and a few days later, while walking to the bus stop I saw him outside.

He appeared out of nowhere like he would so often do. He took his hand and squeezed the back of my neck so tight that I couldn't even see straight. I was scared, and I told him I was only saying I was going to tell but I wasn't.

We got on a bus; I didn't know what was about to happen. I just knew he was mad! Another thing I knew and that was to "fix my face" meaning smile and act like nothing was wrong. We got off the bus and walked down a hill. He took me to a local hotel on Lanham-Severn Road and I don't have any recollection of what happened there nor, do I have any remembrance of how I got home. I don't want to remember it either.

As I grew up, I would cringe every time I travelled on that road. I still get the creeps till this day.

Months later, my menstrual cycle was still a no-show. Because I knew that I better not tell on him, my mind was scrambling as to who I was going to say got me pregnant. Then I figured that I'd make myself believe none of this was really happening.

Meanwhile, there goes the nightmares. I would wake up in the middle of the night and ask the Lord, why am I having nightmares about my biological father's oldest son having sex with me and why am I so little in them. I just assumed it was him because I had never had sex before. The nightmares would always show me as a little girl and a larger man on top of me, but I could never see the face. It had gotten so bad that when I woke up from it and fell back to sleep, it would continue where it left off.

Those nightmares continued for months; until one day I woke up and realized that it was not only a nightmare but that it occurred in real life. I would sit and try and figure out how my biological father's oldest son could have done this to me when I was little, and we had just met when I was 14 years old. That's when I started to realize that it wasn't him after all and I began to pray and ask God to reveal the face to me. I could see the act happening, but the face was blurred.

Finally, God allowed me to see it was my uncle. It was my uncle who always treated me as his favorite niece. He was also the uncle who nicknamed me Bones because I was so skinny. After his face was revealed, the whole abuse by my uncle was revealed as well. I remember it starting under the age of 6 and I do not remember at what age my uncle stopped molesting me.

I do remember, however, being outside playing and he would call my name and I would pretend not to hear him and someone else would tell me that he's calling me. He would then yell at me saying he knows that I heard him and would fuss at me. I would have to stop playing to come inside and ask what he wanted as if I didn't already know.

This one time stands out in my mind. I remember him calling me and I popped my lips thinking, "Not again!" I went inside, and he cracked the bathroom door and told me to go in my grandmother's room and get the Vaseline. I said I didn't want to and he grabbed my arm tightly while twisting it, made this mean face and told me to go and get it. I went in my grandmother's closet to get the Vaseline and hoping I was just going to hand it to him through the cracked door, that wasn't the case.

As I handed it to him, he grabbed me and pulled me through the slightly opened door as well. With newspaper spread on the floor, he laid me down and molested me. When he was done, he first looked out of the bathroom to make sure no one was around and then he sneakily let me out the bathroom to go back outside and play. He then told me that I BETTER NOT tell nobody, or I would get it. I did not tell anybody; I just went back outside as if nothing ever happened.

Years later, around age 12, I recall playing outside in the yard feeling anxious. I was overwhelmed so I told one of my cousins about the sexual abuse my uncle had committed against me. My cousin was a little younger than me. I asked her not to tell anyone and after thinking about my uncle threatening to "get me" if I told anyone, I quickly told her it was a dream just in case she did tell. I didn't want to get in trouble by my uncle.

My cousin told my aunt, her mother. My aunt approached me about it and said, "I heard about that dream you had, humph, that was some dream."

I used to pray and ask God to stop my uncle from hurting me. I used to sit outside of my grandparent's house and wish I could stack houses on top of each other to reach heaven and talk to God about what was going on so that He would make it stop.

That being impossible, I remember writing a letter to God and taking my aunt's matches and burning the letter so that the words would reach heaven. After all, my grandfather did say that we cannot see God because He is a spirit and they that worship Him must worship Him in spirit and in truth. I thought by God not being visible and by me burning the letter, God would be able to interpret it through the smoke.

All I wanted is for the abuse to stop and I forget about it, and eventually that's what happened… I forgot about it along with a whole lot of other things.

The abuse that I suffered by my uncle was long forgotten until my biological father's oldest son started abusing me.

There I was, 15 years old and my nerves were bad. My skin would flare up with small bumps. I'm sure it was because of the pain and suffering I was experiencing. My mother would keep asking what was wrong with me. I dared not to say. My parents took me to see a dermatologist several times and was told it was atopic dermatitis or eczema. The doctor prescribed a cream and it didn't work because I didn't want it to work; I wasn't using it.

While sitting at home crying one day, I remember taking my hands digging my nails in my face, neck, arms and legs as deep as I could, which wasn't that deep because I always bit my nails when I was nervous as a child growing up. Next thing you know, I would grab a brush to make scars because I didn't have nails. That still wasn't good enough because the brush would only make welts and they would soon go away.

Then I decided to get a knife and start cutting my arms, legs, back and other parts of my body within reach. I told myself that I would make my skin look so bad that no one would ever want to take advantage of me again. So, whenever I was anxious about the abuse, I would get a knife and cut myself until I bled. Not enough to kill myself because I didn't want to die…I just wanted the anxiety and pain of what happened to me to go away and somehow that did it.

Most of the time, I walked around in long sleeve shirts and long pants during summer, oftentimes hearing the questions, "Why do you have on those long sleeves?" and "How come you don't ever wear shorts?" My family was thinking I was just ashamed because my skin was so messed up from the "eczema" but really, I was covering up the shame of all that happened to me. I would always say that I was not hot with the long sleeves and laugh it off. Many people just stopped asking and got used to seeing me dress differently.

I remember sitting in the bathroom as I often did, looking myself in the mirror and saying how ugly, dumb and stupid I was and that no one cared for me; after all, that's what I heard most of the time growing up.

One hot day, I remember being around six months pregnant and my parents and I went to the Safeway grocery store on Marlboro Pike. I was so sick. I was in the backseat sweating, feeling weak as if I was about to faint. As my father drove around looking for a parking space, I remember telling him to let me out because I had to use the bathroom badly. I didn't really have to use the bathroom though, I just needed to get out of the car into some air conditioning before I passed out.

When I walked into the store, it felt so good. I began to feel very weak. I could no longer stand. I had to at least find a seat only there were no seats. There was the floor and I laid on it, just inside the automatic doors…trying to regain strength before my father came inside.

People were coming over to me, asking if I was alright and I kept telling them that I was alright. Still lying on the floor, but trying my best to get up, my father came in and started panicking. He kept asking me if I was okay and what happened as he thought I had fallen. I told him that I was alright and that I just needed to rest myself a little bit. I got myself together and he purchased the items we needed.

When we returned to the car, my father told my mother what happened, and he told her that she needed to take me to the hospital because he believed that I was pregnant. I was able to convince my mother otherwise, however.

Now, time was moving right along and so was my pregnancy. I was now seven months pregnant and I haven't told anyone about it because I had better not! That's all I remember. My mother had been asking me for months and I had been lying for months.

She often threatened to take me to the doctor, but I believe she wanted so badly to believe the lie that I was telling her. I believe deep down inside my mother knew I was pregnant. I never even thought about what I was going to tell her when the baby finally came. For now, it wasn't that hard to convince her otherwise, as I was only 100 pounds. So, a few extra pounds here and there weren't *that* noticeable.

Still hoping and praying that God would help me out of the situation and tell me what to do, my big break came. My biological father's oldest son got locked up. Even though he was locked up he would still call and make subliminal threats over the telephone and send me threatening letters. One day, however, I remember him calling and asking me, "You didn't tell your mother, did you?" and at that very moment, I hung up on him and called my Aunt Fannie.

I just remember calling and telling her that I was pregnant. She asked me who I was pregnant by and I told her. She then asked me if I wanted her to call my mother and tell her what happened, and I said yes. She then called and told my mother and my mother screamed at me. "I knew it!", she yelled. She was angry. I told her I was seven months and looking at me she said I couldn't be seven months. She took me to the doctor and I was in fact seven months. It seemed like after I told her, I just blew up out of nowhere.

I never told my mother about all the abuse and everything that happened because in my naïve mind, I thought that he could somehow still be my brother without him trying to do bad things to me. That was absurd but, hey, I was just a child and I thought as a child. Besides, that's what usually happened in my family...everything went right back to "normal" after the abuse.

I did tell her, however, that he kept threatening me and that's why I couldn't tell. I remember he called from jail and after accepting the call I handed the telephone to my mother and she laid him out! I was in the background listening with my eyes wide open thinking, "Wow! That's good she's getting on him!"

Two weeks after turning 16 years old, I gave birth to my son. A couple of weeks later I found out he was born with a chronic blood disorder called sickle cell disease (SS). I wondered what that was. The doctor gave me a lot of material to read and what to expect from the disease. The material was so depressing that

I had to stop reading and I threw it away. I was told that children sometimes didn't live long with this disease.

Now, here I am living with all this abuse, no self-esteem, laughing when I want to cry, a baby with a chronic blood disorder, family members talking badly about me, blaming me, telling anyone who would listen that "Tanya had a baby by her brother."

Anytime there was an argument between me and another person in my family, their final words were, "At least I didn't have a baby by my brother!" All that did was make me recount all the hurt and abuse I had suffered.

I didn't even want to go to Landover Mall because my son's father's girlfriend worked there. It seemed like every time I went to the mall, she was working at a jewelry store. One time, I was walking by, I heard her say, "There she goes...that B (curse word) had a baby with her own brother." Whenever I went shopping at the mall, she or her friends would say, "There she goes…" or ask, "Isn't that her?" I tried to avoid them at all cost. I hated to walk on the end of the mall where she worked.

It bothered me to no end how she was so angry with me and somehow blamed me for being in the situation. I wondered how she could have married this man after knowing what he did to me?

I remember thinking, "I am young now. I'm just a kid. When I grow up, she won't say anything to me then because I'll be able to defend myself."

I felt like I hardly had any peace. If it wasn't for family members talking about me having a baby with my brother, I would still be dealing with him threatening me. Even though his threats didn't bother me too much, I had the constant reminder of what happened to me every time my son got sick. He was in pain starting at the age of three weeks old and cried most of the time.

My grandmother babysat him while I was in school. I had to eventually drop out of school because it was too overwhelming for her to babysit him being in pain all the time because of the chronic blood disorder. I did, however, return to school a year later and I went on to graduate from high school. I was determined to get my high school diploma, find employment, and make a better life for my son than the one I had.

One time my son got sick, I remembered reading a scripture in the Bible about having faith as a grain of a mustard seed. I realized in order for me to have that kind of faith, I had to first figure out what a mustard seed was. After seeing it, I asked God, that's it? I can definitely believe for that little bit and it was so.

In every situation, I began to eat the meat and throw the bones away! I remember reading in the Bible that I should give thanks in every situation, so I would thank God for everything knowing that it was working together for my good. I started looking over my life and all that happened to me and began to give God thanks for allowing me to make it through. I would say, "Lord, I don't know how this is working for my good, but

You are the Word and the Word is You and You are not a man that You should lie, so I thank You!" Then there were those times I told God that I didn't see any sign of goodness, but I have faith and I'll wait.

I hated thinking about the criticism my son would have to endure because of what happened to me. I didn't tell him exactly what happened but something like it minus the abuse. I told him that I met his father at the skating rink and didn't know our relation until after he was born.

Acting as if nothing ever happened had now become part of what I did. Sweeping things under the rug and pretending not to see the abuse that I've seen and experienced had become "normal" just as I saw growing up.

Because I never told my son what had really occurred, he wanted a relationship with his father so, I tried to make it happen. I never spoke bad of his father to him, even though he only visited him once out of the numerous times he was hospitalized. His father stood him up many times and never gave me any money for child support, until the court finally ordered him to pay $50 a month. It was unfortunate because he was a successful barber. His clothes stayed fresh and when he picked up and dropped off my son, he was driving a nice Cadillac Escalade, but wouldn't help me financially.

My son's father continued to make threats against me here and there and I would pay him no mind. I was no longer controlled by his threats.

One day, I got a call from my grandfather. He told me to come to their (my grandparents) house because he wanted to talk to me. When I walked into my grandfather's room, there sat my son's father. My grandfather told me that he had just talked with him about some things. I'm sitting there thinking he may have gone to him for guidance on repentance, so I asked, "What things?"

My grandfather told me that my son's father told him that he wanted to marry me. I told my grandfather that I did not want to marry him. Then my grandfather said there was nothing wrong with it and that we were going to get married and that he was going to marry us. After all, he said, "Abraham and Sarah were brother and sister and they were married."

I told my grandfather again that I did not want to marry my brother (son's father) and plus Mama would not allow me to get married and he said he would handle her.

Because I had seen my grandfather officiate weddings before, I thought he was going to force me into marrying my brother (son's father) right then and there. I remember feeling very afraid…I was about to cry.

Not being disrespectful to my grandfather because I didn't want to get in trouble, but as he continued to talk to me about God and the Bible and why it was such a good idea for me to marry my own brother (son's father), I just remember tuning him out and not hearing anything that was being said to me. I began praying in my mind that God would get me out of there. I got out of there and I got out unmarried.

As I walked back home, I remember thinking, "Abraham and Sarah can be all the married brother and sister they want to be, but I don't want to be married to my brother (son's father)."

After that situation, I began to recollect when I was a very young child, I witnessed my grandfather trying to sexually abuse one of my aunts against her will. My aunt was begging him to stop and he overpowered her.

My aunt drank a lot of wine; she was drunk most of the time. I believe it was to help her cope with the sexual and physical abuse she suffered at the hands of my grandfather, her step-father.

During her drunkenness, she would blurt out things using nasty and inappropriate language to describe what my grandfather had done to her. This sometimes occurred during our church services. My grandfather would plead the Blood of Jesus against her and say things like she had the devil in her. He would try and make her out to be a liar but most of us sitting there knew what she was saying was the truth.

My grandfather would also raise his voice and his hand as if he was going to slap her to prevent her from further speaking on the abuse. She, like a lot of us, was afraid of him.

I began to wonder if my mother was a victim of his abuse as well. My mother was loving, and she loved me, but she has never said the words, "I love you" to me and as a matter of fact, I had never heard her say it at all. If she ever made a statement about love, it would be something like, "You all know that I love you." My mother has never been affectionate. There were no hugs before going to school or when I came home. In fact, there were no hugs or affection at all, ever.

There were times we'd be at church and Bishop would say, "Hug your neighbor." We would hug, but even that felt weird because we had never hugged before. I could feel the void between us. However, as I got older I felt like I'd rather have her show me that she loved me and not say it rather than say she loved me and not show it in her actions.

I feel like I missed out on that part of my life growing up, but I never held it against her because I believe something happened to her and caused her to be that way.

Over the years, I would hear some of Mama's siblings joking about her and her ways. They would say things like, "Your mother does not like hugs…she doesn't let anyone hug her…she has some strange ways." My thoughts were, "Well if your father sexually and physically abused you like I saw him do to her sister, you might have some strange ways too."

My mother has never gone into detail with me about the abuse she suffered as a child at the hands of my grandfather; the man who raised her after her biological father died when she was an infant. However, she would always refer to him as being a nasty man and growing up I was told to stay away from him.

I tried to stay away from him but sometimes he would make me give him a hug and as I resisted he would chuckle and pull me in closer, asking, "You love your granddaddy, don't you?" I hated that! I also hated those nasty wet kisses he'd give me. Yuck!

Not to mention the time he called me downstairs into his bedroom and I walked in but didn't see him. He then told me to come over near the kitchen/bathroom area. When I walked over there, he stood up and was naked. I felt very unsafe. I lied and told him that Mama was waiting on me and I ran out of there. He chuckled and said, "That's alright pudding head, I'll get you."

For those reasons and the way that my mother behaves, I would bet my bottom dollar that my grandfather did in fact abuse my mother as well.

Seeing my grandfather preach and teach God's Word and then commit such heinous acts against my aunt and hearing of other monstrous acts he committed against other family members changed the way I felt about him, but not the way I felt about God! My grandfather chose to do the things that he did. I understand by the Word of God that we all fall short of His Glory and none of us are without sin, so I am not judging him. I am only stating how my grandfather's actions have grossly and directly affected me and my upbringing.

With that being said, it is of great importance that we put our trust in God. Establish a personal relationship with Him. He is our **source**; anyone and anything else is a resource. God uses man as an instrument to teach us His Word, but we must study the Word to show thyself approved. In all your reading, be sure you have understanding.

8

New Beginning

It was 1992 and I had just gotten my first job after scoring 100% on the OPM, U.S. Office of Personnel Management, Civil Service exam. Not only that, my big brother bought me my first car. I was so excited about the new chapter in my life, as I could now afford to take care of myself and my son, as needed.

When I started my new position, I met with my Director, her Deputy Director and told them my son was born with sickle cell disease (SS), a chronic blood disorder. I explained to them that he has experienced many pain crises and hospitalizations because of the disease. I also mentioned that the pain crises can happen anytime, without warning, sometimes he would require medical attention and I would have to take him to his appointments for treatment.

My Director and her Deputy Director were both married women with children. I expected some compassion from the ladies, however, that was not the case most times.

My son was sick more often than not. I had to take off from work many days to care for him, which had me in a leave without pay (LWOP) status most of the time.

My Director would tell me I needed to have another family member take my son to the hospital instead of taking off all the time. I explained to her that I didn't have anyone else to take him and besides when my son was sick he wanted me there with him.

I remember one of my son's many admissions into Holy Cross Hospital and I went to visit him every day. After working from 8:15 a.m. – 5:00 p.m., I would drive directly to the hospital. Usually, I would try and leave the hospital before midnight but sometimes I would be there until 2 a.m. or later, depending on how he was feeling. Then, I would drive home, get a couple of hours of sleep and do it all over again the next day.

One day, my younger brother asked if he could ride with me to the hospital to visit. So, I picked him up when I got off work and we headed over there. As we travelled the beltway in rush hour traffic, I remember staying in the far-right lane because I wanted to take my time. Not realizing I was exhausted from working and staying late hours at the hospital every day, I dozed off. When I woke up, we were merging into the far-left lane. I yelled, "Oh my God!"

My younger brother then woke up asking what happened and I said to him, "You're over there asleep!" Then I told him that I had fallen asleep as well. We both were wide awake after that. I thank God for watching over us and not allowing me to cause hurt or harm to anyone, including my younger brother or myself. God kept me and my younger brother.

The next day, I took off from work because I needed some rest. When I returned to work, I met with my Director and her Deputy Director and told them about how I had fallen asleep on my way to visit my son at the hospital. I also asked if they could have someone help me with the project I was working on because I could not stay after hours to get it done. I was denied assistance and told that what I was going through with my son was personal.

After my son was discharged, he continued to get sick and I had no choice but to take off or come in to work late. I received a memo from my Director stating that I was being placed on leave restriction because of my frequent unscheduled absences from work. I tried explaining to her that I do not schedule when my son gets sick. If I could control things, I would make sure he never did get sick, but that was not the case.

The pain crises happened out of nowhere. I told her my only choice was to use unscheduled leave. I continued to take off with my son as needed and before long I was placed on absent without leave (AWOL).

One year, my son was extremely ill. He was being hospitalized for an extended amount of time and I was required to stay with him.

I told my Director what was going on and she told me to get something in writing from the doctor. So, I gave her the letter. She read the letter from the doctor and said that they need to provide more information. The doctor wrote another letter being as detailed as possible; it was on hospital letterhead and there was also a telephone number for her to call him directly, if she needed more information.

My Director still said that she needed more information. The doctor told me he was not writing any more information than the one-page letter he had already written, and she finally accepted it.

During the weeks in which I was scheduled to be absent from work, my Director told me that I had to call in everyday at 8:15 a.m. to let her know I was not coming in. Calling in to the office every morning when she already knew I was not coming in made no sense to me. When I questioned her about it, I was told, "In order for the request for LWOP to be approved, you are required to call in everyday at 8:15 a.m." If I did not call in at 8:15 a.m. each day, I would be placed on AWOL.

I called into the office every morning at 8:15 a.m. I recall calling in and she would answer the telephone and say, "Tanya, it's not 8:15 a.m., you need to call back." Un-freakin-believable! I tried to explain to her that according to my clock it was 8:15 a.m. but again was told to call back. I waited a couple of minutes and called back. When I called back my Director told me that it was 8:17 a.m. and that she was placing me on AWOL.

That was a very emotional time for me. My son was very ill, I was exhausted from being up with him all night and if that wasn't enough, I was dealing with my Director's unconscionable request. I remember sitting there praying, crying, and stressing, asking God when I would finally catch a break.

I worked in a non-bargaining unit and there was no union. I decided to contact Human Resources regarding the unfair treatment I was receiving and there was nothing they would do about it. I read all the memoranda I received regarding being placed on LWOP, AWOL, and leave restriction. As I continued reading, silently praying "Lord, I am going to save these papers because one day I am going to look back and thank you for delivering me, once again."

In 1999, our agency was consolidated into the State Department. Before relocating, my Director and her Deputy Director met with me and said that our office was going over as a whole; however, I wasn't going to be a part of their group. In my mind, I said, "Thank you, Jesus!" They told me that I would be going into a new office with all new people. "They are way stricter over there," is what they said.

I was being told that I would not be able to take off with my son. I felt like they were trying to intimidate me. After all the negative talk, my Deputy Director asked me what I thought about having to go over there not knowing anyone and not being with our group. I smiled and told her that I was looking forward to it. I also told her that change would be good.

A lot of times I felt like my Director and her Deputy Director went out of their way to give me a hard time. For instance, everyone had visitors to our office whether it was a spouse (not my Director and her Deputy Director, their husbands never came to visit in the seven years I worked with them), companion or friend. When my husband came to visit on Mondays, there was always a problem. They would ask me why he comes every week for lunch and where he works that affords him the flexibility to come have lunch with me.

Then, I was told that the lunch he was bringing me was a problem. My Director told me it smells good, but it smells up the whole office and suggested that my husband bring me lunch on Fridays when our staff usually ordered carry out. She knew that was impossible because we had already discussed him being off on Mondays only.

My Director then told me that he could no longer have lunch with me because he didn't have a security clearance. When I told her that we would continue having lunch, we would just have lunch outside of the office, she told me I needed to eat at my desk in case something urgent came up.

Then, there were the issues with the way I dressed. My Director wanted to know why I always wore black. I remember one time I was leaving out of the Deputy Director's office and she called out to me. When I returned, she said to me, "Um, Tanya, could you *please* (emphasis on please) stop wearing those pants because they make me dizzy?" Usually, I would ignore the many foolish things that were said to me, but I was tired of it. I told her maybe if she would stop watching me so hard, she wouldn't get dizzy. It was always something with those two women. I looked forward to a new beginning.

I started my new position at the State Department and it was nothing like I heard it would be. God blessed me to work with a great group of people.

Having gone through so much at my former job, I was self-conscious about a lot of things including my look and style of dress. Also, I was hesitant to talk about my son and his health issues. My new Director and supervisor were very understanding, however. I would tell them the school had called and that I needed to leave early because my son was sick. They would say, “Alright, we’ll see you tomorrow.” When I didn’t come into work because he was sick, they would say, “Alright, we hope he feels better.”

I would go on and on explaining every single detail because that’s what I was used to doing and I was told my doctor’s note was sufficient.

There was so much kindness shown to me that I sometimes thought it was a trick; I was not used to being treated that way.

God truly blessed me to work with a great group of people. They genuinely cared about me and my son. It was a huge blessing having peace of mind in the workplace while dealing with the stress of caring for my chronically ill son.

9

Overcoming

One day, a friend of mine had been hanging out at our house and before leaving, I asked if I could keep his cap because I really liked it. Not long after, there was a knock on the door, I thought it was him and maybe he changed his mind and needed his cap. I peeped out the window and saw that it was my son's father. He saw me too. He started banging on the door and yelling for me to open the door. I was frantic!

He was banging on the door so hard that I could see the door shake with each pound! I was afraid! I asked what he wanted because I didn't think he was there to visit my son as he hadn't visited him in a long time. He kept yelling for me to open the door and shouted, "I know your mother and them are not here!" "Open the door!"

I called my aunt who lived with my grandparents about six houses up the street from us. She came down in a hurry. Trying to assure me that only she would come inside, she asked me to open the front door. I was crying and in fear, telling her that I can't open the door because he's going to force his way in too.

He kept shouting, "Tanya, open the door! I'm not going to do anything to you."

I was insisting that I knew that he was going to try to hurt me. I asked him why he was here?! He said that he just wanted to tell me something but would not tell me through the door. He then said he would go on the side of my mother's house so that I could let my aunt inside. He did. I went to the side door and looked out the window and there he stood.

I returned to the front door and asked my aunt if she was sure he was still on the side. She assured me that he was. He even shouted from the side and said, "Tanya, I'm on the side!" I told my aunt she needed to move quickly inside, and I opened the door.

He quickly came around the side of the house, hopped a fence and bust in the door. I don't know how he managed to move that quickly, but he did. He then choked me so hard, I could literally see things start to fade to black… all I remember is counting down and then just before going out, he stopped. He ripped a chain from my neck, took the cap that I had been wearing and said, "I'll take that…thanks!" He put the cap on his head and left.

I never told my mother because I just felt like it was somehow my fault, as usual.

As time went on, I realized that I didn't have to be cordial with my son's father. In fact, I didn't have to deal with him at all. I stopped answering his calls. I prayed for him, the situation and hoped for things to get better for my son's sake.

Meanwhile, because of his absence from my son's life, I found myself overcompensating. I would buy my son everything he wanted. The one thing he wanted, however, was time with his father and his paternal side of the family. That, I couldn't buy. I wanted to tell him so badly what the truth about us was, but I wouldn't as it would only make things worse.

My son was already acting out, getting into trouble in school, lying, stealing and doing whatever he could to get attention. The only problem was that he wasn't getting the attention that he wanted… from his father.

After several attempts to have my son's child support of $50/month increased, we eventually went back to court because $50/month was not nearly enough for me to provide for my son. I remember my son's father hired this "big time" attorney who was well-known at the court house. I thought to myself, "Oh, you can hire an attorney, but you can't pay me more than $50/month. I said, "Lord, I need you to grant me favor with the judge."

My court appointed attorney called me into a room and told me that my son's father offered to increase the child support to $75/month and suggested that I accept it. I declined. She advised me that it was a good offer and that it was more than he was paying currently. I declined again, and I told her that I had lots to tell the judge.

My court appointed attorney informed me that I would be in front of the judge but would not be doing any of the talking. She said she would do all the talking for me. I knew I was in big trouble. I left out of her presence and sat on a bench, talking to God about all that was happening.

Then, I saw and overheard my son's father talking to his attorney saying that they need to hurry up because he needed to get back to work. His attorney went inside the courtroom and

I'm not sure what happened, but the next thing I knew, our names were being called.

His attorney stated his case and my court appointed attorney wasn't saying anything that I asked her to say. So, I began to talk over her and the judge allowed me to state my own case. She allowed me to say all that I needed to say, and I was granted $400+ a month.

My son's father was livid! If his eyes had bullets, he would have shot me. When our case was over, I asked the court if they would please keep him inside to give me enough time to get to my car and drive off, as I was afraid of what he would do to me. I ran out of there nervous and shaking all the way to my vehicle.

My son's father remained absent from his life for a long time. I continued to pray and ask God to intervene in that situation. Eventually, he started calling and spending time with my son. He invited him to stay overnight at his house. I was so happy to see my son finally getting what he had always wanted…a relationship with his father. After all, it wasn't his fault, why should he have to suffer. He suffered enough with his health.

Time went on and I got even stronger in the Word of God. Instead of being angry at my son's father, I began to pray for him. The Bible says in Hebrews 1:13 that "God will make your enemies your footstool." He said in Matthew 5:44 that "I should pray for those who spitefully used me" and so I did. I prayed that God would change my son's father's heart.

I prayed that he would have a relationship with my son and do right by him. My son's father's behavior changed. He started showing up when he said he would. He started allowing my son to spend weekends at his home. He even allowed him to live with him and his wife for a time. Prayer sure did change things.

As for me, I spoke to him when necessary, for issues or information to be shared about our son.

In 2002, my son's father called me on his own birthday. When he called, I remember looking at the telephone saying to myself, "What is this fool calling me for?" He knew my son wasn't home from school yet and I wondered what he wanted. I initially wasn't going to answer the telephone but changed my mind and answered.

He asked how I was doing and I told him that I was fine. He told me that my son is always talking about how we go to church all the time. I was very short with him because I really had nothing to say. He then said, "Yea, he also told me how y'all be putting all that money in church." I said, "Yep, when you give, it will be given back to you." He said, "Tanya, you don't know what them people do with all that money" and I told him that it's not for me to know.

I explained to him that The Bible says in Malachi 3:8-10 that "we are to bring our tithes and offerings into the storehouse." I told him The Bible also says in Philippians 4:19 that "God will supply my every need" and He has been doing that. I began to tell him that I believe when you give, it doesn't necessarily mean you are going to get it back in money and material things.

It could be improving your health. So I don't care what they do with it; I'm doing what I'm supposed to do.

He then said, "I'm going to start going to church too." I said, "That's good…you should." He then said with a chuckle, "I'm going to also put in an offering." I said, "That's good too!" He then said, "I'm going to put in $10 and ask them to give me my $9.75 change." We both laughed.

He told me that he just wanted to call and tell me he's sorry for all the stuff he did to me. He asked, "Can you forgive me?" I told him that I forgave him, and he then thanked me and asked me to have my son call him when he gets home from school. I ended the call by saying, "Happy birthday!" He said, "Thanks! That just made my day!" I said, "You're welcome." and we hung up.

After that conversation, I remember saying to myself, "Thank you Jesus! Things are looking better, and everything is going to be alright!"

That night, my husband and I went to a special service at church. My son stayed at my mother's house and I told her we would pick him up afterwards. What happens next is kind of hard to explain. During the service, as I sat there it seemed like my son's father came in the church, it was so weird. It was like he was there but not there because I could no longer see him, but I could hear him.

This sounds crazy, but I heard him say, “See, Tanya, I did come.” I thought to myself that I had better snap out of it and wondered what was wrong with me.

Shortly after that, my mother came to the church and as I looked over to my right, I could see her whispering something to my husband. My first thought was my son must be sick and I must go and pick him up.

They told me to come out into the vestibule as they had something they needed to tell me. I was very worried and wondered what it was? Come to find out, my son’s father was shot and killed. My mother needed me to pick up my son, take him home and explain to him what had just happened.

What a difficult thing that was for me to do. It seemed like my son finally had the relationship he always wanted and now his father was dead and gone.

I thank God for forgiveness. I thank God for blessing me to have an open heart and mind to answer the telephone when my son’s father called.

After his passing, I sent out an email asking my family members to please keep my son in prayer. My aunt, who was also my son’s godmother, then sent out an email to a group of people stating that she would also keep me and my big brother in prayer as not only was he my son’s father but he was also my brother.

I was upset about what she did, but I wasn’t surprised as she was known to be messy and start confusion. Her sister-in-law once described her as “hopelessly miserable and one who unremorsefully gallivants with married men and then brags about it.”

At my son’s father’s funeral, I read the obituary and his wife listed my son’s name along with his other children. She also included my name as his sister and my husband’s name in parentheses. My first thought was, “Wow, she wanted to announce one last time that I had a baby by my brother.” I thought about it and smiled to myself saying, thank God I am no longer controlled by what people think of me. I remember thanking God for deliverance of abuse and my abusers.

Shortly after those programs were handed out, I received another obituary. That one had a picture of my son’s father, his girlfriend and their two-year-old son on the front of it. When I looked over at the wife, she had a look of disgust on her face. I just shook my head and said to myself, “See you must do unto others as you would have them to do unto you.”

10

The Lock Up

One cold evening, I was laying in my bed, watching TV and my telephone rang. It was my cousin. She told me that she was at our aunt's house and invited me to come over because they were going to Pentagon City mall.

My first response was to decline because I wanted to stay in the house and finish watching TV. As we talked longer, she began telling me that she and a few others were at the house and that I should come down and hang out for a little bit. I then asked her, so what exactly are y'all doing, and she said just talking and listening to music. I said, "Alright I'll see you when I get there." and we hung up.

My aunt lived approximately three minutes away from our house. I got up and began to put on my boots. As I sat on my bed looking around, I noticed a bag of trash. My mother could not stand for us to have trash in our bedrooms. She wanted us to not only keep our bedrooms clean but the whole house clean.

Looking at the trash bag, I could hear a small still voice saying, "Don't go." It was like a warning. Feeling confused, I looked around the room wondering, "Hmmmm…what was that?" Again, I heard, "Don't go" in like a hurtful kind of tone. It's very hard to explain. I started feeling like something bad was going to happen but told myself, "I must be tired…I am tripping."

I stood up and took my coat out the closet. Looking at myself in the mirror, I wondered what all that "don't go" stuff was all about? As I reached for the doorknob in my bedroom, I looked at the bag of trash again, grabbed it and said to myself, "I better get this trash out of here just in case something does happen to me, so Mama won't be mad." Even after having all those thoughts that I should not go, I still left out of the house.

I arrived at my aunt's house and we sat around talking, laughing, joking, and dancing. I said to my aunt, "It's getting late and asked what time we are going to the mall as it will probably be closing soon." She told me we'd be leaving soon. That was fine.

A few of us went into the kitchen to eat snacks and we sat at the table, talking and joking around. More time had passed and now I'm thinking we're probably not going to the mall, so I got up from the table and got a few more carrots out of the refrigerator. As I sat with my back to the living room where my aunt and cousin was, I heard this big boom, a very loud noise that scared me. It sounded like something extremely heavy fell.

I looked to my right but by then the person sitting to my right who could see into the living room area hopped out of his seat, yelling, "It's the police!" and ran to the back door, which was in the kitchen. I was thinking, "What in the world is going on?!" Now, I had seen a show called "Cops" enough to know and I remember hearing them say, "Nobody moves…nobody gets hurt…" so I stayed planted in my seat, eating my carrot. My first thought was, "Lord, please don't let them shoot us!"

As a person ran and opened the back door which I was facing, all I saw were police officers rushing in wearing black from head to toe, holding assault rifles in their hands. I remained seated with my elbows on the table, both hands up and visible. My empty left hand raised, and my right hand raised holding a carrot. I still did not move until one of the officers shouted, “Ma’am, get on the floor!” I said, “I’m down” and rolled right out of my seat and onto the floor.

I didn’t push away from the table, I didn’t try to stand up, I rolled to the right and hit the floor. As the officer stood there with the tip of his big black boot to my nose and an assault rifle pointed at me, I closed my eyes and began to tell God how sorry I was for not adhering to His warnings earlier. I said, “Lord, you told me not to go. You even told me a second time and I still did not listen, but I tell you on this day, whatever you tell me to do from now on…I will do it. God, you do not have to worry about me not listening again.”

A sense of peace came over me and I felt like God was with me and He heard my cry. I asked God again to please not let me get shot. After that, they put these tight twist ties on my wrists and sat me up. Me being naïve to getting in trouble with the law, I asked the officer, “Excuse me, can I please have the real handcuffs because these things are hurting my wrist” as if they were really concerned about me being uncomfortable. As time went on, I began to hear what was going on. I heard the officers talking about drugs and guns.

I started to worry and ask God to please help me as I know nothing about any of this. I told God I only came down here to go to the mall and buy jeans. I could hear someone talking about us going to jail and I remember praying to God and telling Him that I cannot go to jail…I haven't done anything. I must raise my son. I am all he has.

There is no one who will take him to the doctor and stay with him at the hospital when he's sick. Oh God, I said, please don't let him get sick while I'm there. I began to cry, thinking my son may be wondering where I was and why I hadn't gotten home yet. I wished I had never left the house.

I remember a police officer taking me outside and placing me in his police cruiser. There were many people outside, so I knew someone would tell my mother what happened and that she would come and get me. I went to the local jail and I remember going into this room with a female officer. She told me to get undressed, pull my underwear down, bend over, spread my butt cheeks and cough.

I felt humiliated. I was also embarrassed because when I had removed all my clothes, I knew that she would see all the scars that I had on my body that I always kept covered. I wondered what she would think of me. Even though I didn't know her, I cared about what she thought. I asked the officer if that was really necessary for me to show my body and she said that it was, so I did.

The next thing I know, they had us all in a jail cell together, except my aunt. I looked around the cell one time and said to myself, "No one better not say one word to me! I will never go to my aunt's house again…EVER!" I was upset about being in jail. I was worried about my son and I was wondering what was taking my mother so long to pick me up?

I remember sitting there praying and asking God to help me to get out of jail because I needed to be there for my son. Then, I remember an officer coming into the cell and taking me out. I thought my mother was there to pick me up. She was not. I asked them had she even called, and they said that she hadn't called.

I was taken to the commissioner, I believe, and there was an officer standing to my right. The commissioner asked me questions about why I was at my aunt's house and I told him I was going to the Gap with her and my cousin. He also asked where and with who do I live with. He also asked questions about the things they said were found in the house and I told him that I didn't know what he was talking about. I reiterated to him that I was at home laying down when my cousin called me and said they were going to the mall, I said I would go and that was it.

I then explained to them that I really need to get home to my son as I am the only person he has. The officer then told me to, "Just tell him that you won't do it again and we'll let you go home." I said, "I'm not saying I won't do anything again, because I didn't do anything." Next thing I know, they took me back to the cell and then later I was given some paperwork and was told I could leave. Thank God!

I called my mother to let her know that I was released, and my father came to pick up my cousin and I; he brought us home. The ride home was quiet. The only thing I was concerned about was seeing my son and hoped he knew nothing about what was going on. As we approached home and we passed by my aunt's house, I remember thinking, "I will never step foot back in that place again! As a matter of fact, I think I'll start going another way to and from home just so I won't even have to look at it and be reminded of this entire ordeal."

We arrived at the house after midnight; it was now Sunday. I had a few hours to sleep because I was getting up and going to church. I told myself that I needed to go to church and get help from the Lord. The morning came and as I got dressed for church, I remember thinking, "I sure hope so and so preaches today because I'm in trouble and I need a Word from the Lord." Whenever he preached, it was always on time for whatever I was going through.

So, we went and there was another person preaching. I remember saying to myself, "Oh, no! Why is he preaching? He's not going to preach like so and so." Well, I quickly snapped out of it and said, God can use anybody to deliver His Word and I sat there with expectancy.

Now the sermon was not about what I was going through, however, when he made an alter call for prayer, his exact words were, "if you need a doctor, God can be your doctor, if you need a lawyer, He can be your lawyer" and I don't know what else he said after that because I jumped out of my seat and ran down to the alter as fast as I possibly could, praising and worshipping God until I was laid out in the floor.

When I woke up, I had a message from God and it was, "Everything is going to be alright." I was also told to go back to my aunt's house, where I was arrested and give her a message. My first thought was, "I don't want to go there, but I must do what thus saith the Lord." I arrived at her house and knocked on the front door. She opened it and greeted me with a hug.

As I walked in, I noticed and could hear my uncle who had molested me, continuing his conversation with my aunt as he sat in a chair. "I'm not here to stay," I said, "but I just came home from church with a message from God to you." She said, "Okay, what is it?" I told her that He told me to tell you to "turn from your wicked ways and He would make everything alright and that you will not go to jail." She then said, "Tanya, I don't know."

My uncle then chimed in saying, "Nah shawty, I heard it was a lot of stuff in here, y'all gonna do some time." She was looking rather sad, of course. I then told her again what God had told me and that she should just do what God said.

My uncle interrupted once again saying "I'm telling you, somebody going to jail, they said there were drugs and guns and stuff up in here; somebody is going to jail." In that very moment, I remember thinking that perhaps it will be him going to jail for what he did to me. I said my goodbye. My work was done. I did what God told me to do.

He said to deliver the message, not convince anyone to believe it. That part was up to her. I believed what God said. I did not hang around to hear about all the stuff "they" said was found in the house or how much time in jail "they" would get because that had absolutely nothing to do with me.

Our court date arrived. As I entered the courtroom, I saw everyone who was in the house on the day of our arrest. I sat with my cousin and her mother. Each person was called separately as they read each charge. I heard something about some people being prosecuted and they would receive a follow-up court date.

However, when they called my name, I clearly remember the judge reading all the charges against me and someone saying, "We do not wish to prosecute her." The judge said I could go and then just as I turned to walk away, he called me back up there and asked about one other charge and I heard someone say, "We do not wish to prosecute her." I was praising God all day long! God is so good! Once again, He kept me.

Now that clean slate didn't come without a whole lot of bad talk about me. There were rumors going around that I must have said something to someone or paid somebody…along with a host of other lies. I wondered what I could have possibly said about anyone when I didn't know anything to tell anyone.

Another thing, there were people who always talked about God and how much they believed in Him, but when He brought me out, many could not believe it. There was a lot of "Girl, how did you do that?" Even when I answered it was not me, it was God. I would hear, well I know it was God, but you had to do something.

When God kept me, some of my family members disassociated themselves from me. I was hurt. It was very hard to understand why, even though they knew that I had never been involved in any illegal activities.

In the end, after the trials, no one including my aunt, went to jail.

11

Pregnancy

In the year 2000, I remember having blood work done and finding out my husband and I were expecting a baby. We scheduled an appointment to see the doctor. I remember sitting there feeling quite excited about it until an ultrasound was done and they didn't see anything. I was sent back to the lab to have more blood work drawn. The numbers had increased since the last visit, however, nothing was seen on the ultrasound.

I went home and returned in a couple days and my blood levels were checked again. This time a transvaginal ultrasound was done and there was no baby in the womb. I had an ectopic pregnancy with twins. The babies were in my left tube. Everything moved pretty quickly at that point. I was immediately scheduled to have a surgery to have the tube removed.

My husband and I headed to Holy Cross hospital and there the surgery was performed. I was discharged home the same day. I followed up with a visit to my doctor's office and she told me that my left tube was badly damaged, so it had been removed. She said the other one was just as badly damaged, but they had not removed it. I breathed a sigh of relief.

My doctor then told me that I would not be able to have any more children. When I questioned her, she explained that with the tube being as bad as it was, getting pregnant again would only end in either another ectopic pregnancy or a miscarriage. I looked at that woman and said, "I don't receive anything negative spoken over my life." She was looking at me as if I was crazy and slowly repeated what she had just told me. I then told her that while I understand she is the doctor and this is what she does, God made me, and He could fix me. She said, "Alright, I'm just telling you" and I said, "And I'm just telling you."

I left her office upset and disturbed. I sat in the car crying and went home.

Later that year, we continued to try to conceive. I was so elated when I discovered that I was pregnant! The first thing that I did was thank God. I also realized that the doctor's predictions were not applicable to me and that God has the last word.

I was going to my appointments and having blood work done. All was well; everything was going according to plan. I remember sitting in the examination room, waiting for my ultrasound. The doctor said, "Look, see the heart beating!" I was in awe as I had never experienced that before. What an amazing thing it was.

My next scheduled appointment came, and the doctor said the levels were a little low and asked how I had been feeling. I said I was great! She did an ultrasound and we saw something on the screen, but we didn't hear anything. At first, I thought the volume was down but as I looked closely at the screen, there was no movement whatsoever.

I looked over at my doctor and she had this look of concern. I began to feel nervous. She told me I had a missed-miscarriage. I wondered, "What the heck is that?" Feeling like a huge knot was in my throat, I asked, what it was. She told me it is a miscarriage that didn't come out and that I would have to return to the hospital for a dilation and curettage (**D&C**). I almost asked why they have to take it out hoping that it would live again. She explained everything to me, scheduled my appointment and off I went.

I cried all the way to the car. I kept thinking about what she had told me before, that I wouldn't be able to get pregnant and if I did, it would result in another ectopic pregnancy or a miscarriage. I got in my car and I cried. I began to think about what I believe and what I wanted instead of what she said. I shook my head, like one would do with an etch-a-sketch, to erase what I was feeling, and I began to thank God. I apologized to Him for not believing and I said I'm going to continue to trust Him no matter what.

I remember talking to a family member over the phone and she told me that she had heard I was pregnant again. I told her that I had a missed-miscarriage and she said, "You need to just stop telling people you're pregnant." I felt so badly when she said those words to me. There was another family member who said something similar and I told myself that I would continue telling people each time I conceived.

One Sunday while at church, I remember the minister was talking about women having issues getting pregnant and he prayed over some clay that he had. He asked those of us who wanted to and believed that God would restore us to come down. I said a quick prayer as he was talking, and I asked God to restore the tube that was removed and repair the one that was still there. I walked down to the altar and ate the clay. I was initially distracted by the taste of it and what I had just eaten. I immediately told myself that I would not be distracted, and I don't care what it tastes like. I believe that God is going to do just what the minister said He would do if I trusted and believed.

Some time went on and eventually I conceived yet again. Glory be to God! I told everyone about the pregnancy. Of course, there were those that said, "You're pregnant…again?!" There were others who were happy and excited for us.

One day, I was driving home as Kurt Carr's song titled, "I Almost Let Go" played on the radio. As my son and I talked, I could feel the flutters of the baby. Not far from home, out of nowhere, a car crossed the center line and hit us head on. My son was crying and in pain. I was crying and in pain and not only that, I no longer felt the flutters.

My first thought was…not again! Please God, have mercy I asked. I placed my hand on my stomach and moved it across my belly and nothing happened, no flutters. That's unusual to me because there were always flutters whether I touched my stomach or not. When I did touch my stomach, however, there was always an immediate flutter. But this time…nothing.

Someone called my husband and he met us at the hospital. They took me directly to Labor and Delivery. Because I had not felt the flutters all that time, I started to think there was a problem with the baby, once again. I was having a battle in my mind; one part was thinking it's going to be bad news and the other part is believing that the song, "I Almost Let Go" playing in the background was my hope in the situation. The nurse performed a sonogram and I made up in my mind that I would only look at my husband's face for the answer. After all, I could not bear to look at the screen and once again see a heart not beating.

At the last minute, I looked in the opposite direction of my husband. The nurse told me to look at the screen and I would not. My husband told me to look at the screen and I still would not until he said, "Baby look, it's alright." Just as he said that, the nurse said, "Look, the baby is waving!" As I looked at the screen, she was waving her hand. I felt like she was saying, "I'm doing fine, mommy."

God not only blessed me with her in the year 2002, but He blessed me with another baby girl in 2003!

We must be so careful of the things that we accept. Just because someone tells you something, it does not mean it is so. God made us, and He has the capacity to change every situation concerning us.

12

Marriage

We must put God first in everything we do including our marriage. He is the glue that holds it together. No matter how often we attend church services or how active we are in the church, we need God to help us maintain our relationships with one another. I found this out early in my marriage.

My husband Steve and I were both reared in the church and we attended church services regularly. As a matter of fact, I met him in the church.

In the very beginning, I told my husband about the abuse that I suffered. One of the reasons I told him early on is because I did not want him hearing it from anyone else. There was always a cousin or an aunt waiting to tell the matter to anyone who would listen.

I also told him about the abuse because I felt it was necessary for him to understand the affect it had on me. I was extremely distrustful of people, so it was of the utmost importance to me that he be the person he presented himself to be and do the things that he told me he would do.

I also explained to him that I was very vocal. If something was bothering me, I would speak on it whether he wanted to hear it or not. When I felt like a lie was being told, I addressed it. I wasn't gullible. He could not tell me just anything and I was going to believe it.

When we got married, my husband was the breadwinner in the home. He always made more money than I did, and in some instances, he was the only one earning an income.

For that reason, I sometimes felt like he thought he could do what he wanted to do, and he tried it.

It seemed as if he thought because he was paying most of the bills, I had no say so in anything. Well that was just a thought! I still said what I needed to say and didn't care how much money he made.

I also felt Steve was a bit controlling. He would buy me things and when we got into an argument, he would take them away from me. It had gotten to the point that I wouldn't even wait for him to take them back, I'd just hand them over. Material things didn't make me happy anyway.

I told Steve, "one of these days I will have more money than you and then I won't have to worry about you taking things away from me."

During our arguments, it seemed like the more I ignored Steve, the worse he got. Taking things back that he gave me did not impact me emotionally, so he had to find something new and improved.

Meanwhile, I had to keep reminding myself that it wasn't about him, it was about me and my relationship with God. When I thought about what God had done for me and how He had kept me all my life, repaying evil with evil was not an option.

My belief was as long as I am lining up with what God's Word says, the people and things in my life would line up as well. Isaiah 26:3 says, "You will keep in perfect peace all who trust in you, all whose thoughts are fixed on you!" and that's what I believed.

I remember one time while I was at work, we got into an argument over the telephone. Steve told me our marriage was over and he was going to change the locks.

Well, when he said it was over, it was like him saying good morning, he said it often in an effort to control me. When I held him accountable, he'd say it was over. When he didn't get his way, he'd say it was over. When I didn't see things his way, he'd say it was over.

This time, however, he said he was also changing the locks and that is when I took it real seriously. I asked him not to change the locks and he said to me, "I'm telling you, do not go home because I am changing the locks and you are going to be standing outside embarrassed."

Surely, I didn't want to be standing in the hallway of our duplex apartment embarrassed because my key no longer worked. I kept thinking about what my son might say or what the neighbors would say if they saw me.

Then I started wondering if the neighbors had actually seen him change the locks. My mind went into overdrive. I called him a few times, but he would not answer. I wanted to ask him to reconsider his decision, so I called a few more times. Still, no answer.

I began to talk to the Lord, telling Him all that had happened. I expressed my fears and worries to Him. I also told Him that I was only taking up for myself, something I had not done most of my life. I asked God to please let me be able to get in the house. Eventually, I left work and headed home.

Feeling nervous and not knowing what to expect, I decided to stop at my girlfriend Gerbie's house to talk to her about it.

As soon as I told her, she asked, "Tanya, what did you do?" I told her what had occurred, that we had gotten into an argument over the telephone. She said, "Tanya, it has to be something else, was it about another dude, you had to do something because Steve is too nice to do that?" I smiled and said, "You just don't know, love covers a multitude of sins."

I sat there a little longer, hoping by the time I left her house, he would call and say he had a change of heart. That call never came. My girlfriend told me, "girl go on home, I bet he didn't change them locks." It was late, so I agreed that I needed to get home and I left. I prayed all the way home, "Lord, please let me be able to get in."

I arrived home and up the stairs I went to unlock the door. I remember putting the key in and my eyes lit up, then I turned the key and was able to get in! "Thank you, Jesus!!" I shouted while jumping up and down in the hallway.

As I walked inside, I continued to thank God for hearing my prayers. About five minutes later, Steve walked in. I was smiling because I was about to tell him how I had appreciated him not changing the locks, but he appeared to be pissed!

I said, "Hi!" and he didn't even speak. He said, "Yea, I see you called a locksmith" Looking confused, I asked him, "What do you mean, I called a locksmith?" He said, "You heard what I said, you called a locksmith." I said to him, "I didn't call a locksmith." He angrily said, "Yes you did! How did you get into the house?" I then asked in disbelief, "So wait a minute, you *did* change the locks?" He said, "Yes I changed them, you know I changed them!"

I kept insisting that I didn't know anything. Then he walked past me into the kitchen and pulled out the old locks that were changed earlier that day.

I started jumping up and down, giving God the highest praise and told him, "I didn't call a locksmith, I called on Jesus! He is my locksmith! He knew what you did was wrong, and He gave me a master key so any lock you put on, I would still be able to get in!" He stood there amazed. I told him, "God is not going to just let you do to me whatever you think you are big enough to do."

Just thinking about that, made me shout again! Thank you Jesus!

In 2002, only two months after giving birth to our daughter and my son losing his father, my husband and I separated.

Before the separation, Steve would come home sharing stories about people being cheated on by their mates. He then, started acting strange towards me. It seemed like he began to imagine that he was in their shoes.

When I would be sitting on the sofa breastfeeding our daughter, he would come home and say, “I caught you.” He claimed that he was just playing, although I did not find it funny. While Steve kept claiming that he was “just playing,” I noticed that he was planting a seed in his own mind that I was cheating.

He started complaining about me breastfeeding our daughter as it was causing him to feel neglected. I felt that he should have understood that our daughter needed to eat.

Then, he began to have a problem with me spending too much time at my Aunt Fannie’s house. My son loved visiting her, so I thought it would help him cope with the loss of his father.

That’s when he started accusing me of doing things that simply weren’t true. Honestly, I felt maybe Steve wanted to do the things he was accusing me of, or perhaps, he had already been doing them.

He began to hang out all times of the night and would hardly ever be at home to help me with the children, including our newborn. Not to mention, I was not working, had no income and was still suffering with back pain from a car accident. I remember one Sunday morning, he came home around 4 a.m. and I was heated. It was the last straw for me. I told him that his behavior was unacceptable and that something was going to change.

He said that I should leave then, and I told him I wasn’t going anywhere. Then, he said he would leave. He began to tell me which of the furniture and other items he was taking with him and I told him whatever he took was fine. He called his friends over to help him move and I watched them pack up and leave.

As if that wasn't enough, Steve then stopped at our rental office and put in a 30-day notice. He also requested to turn off our electric and have our telephone service disconnected immediately.

I had no idea he was going to do all of that!

What kind of person would want to disconnect our landline, knowing my son (whom he called his son as well) had health issues and I needed a telephone in case of an emergency?

One day our daughter suffered an emergency due to reflux and I had to call 911. When the paramedics entered, one of them looked around and told me that I could just lay her on the kitchen table because we had no other furniture; that was so embarrassing.

I sent text messages to Steve and I also called him several times to tell him about our daughter and he never even answered the telephone.

A few days later, I received a notice from the rental office to vacate the property.

I was very private, and other than my immediate family, I didn't want to tell people what was going on for fear of hearing it was somehow my fault, as I had heard most of my life. I decided to take a chance and tell someone what was happening.

First, I went to the rental office and asked what I needed to do to remain in our duplex apartment. I was told that I probably would not be able to because I had no income. Wrong answer. I wasn't accepting that! I contacted management, explained the situation and was told what I needed to do to stay there.

Secondly, I contacted a friend who helped me tremendously. I thank God for her helping me and with her assistance I was not only able to pay the rent, I was able to pay utilities until I returned to work. Thank You Jesus!

Many times, I was hurt and angry with Steve for abandoning us and I contemplated ways of hurting him that would have broken him down like a fraction, but I didn't go through with any of them.

While he was living it up, I was at home praying for his protection, praying for his business, praying that he would be all that God had intended for him to be. After all, he was my children's father regardless of what was happening between us.

I didn't have a relationship with my biological father. I was around two years old when he died. My mother didn't have a relationship with her biological father; she was eight months old when he died. I wanted to break the cycle. I wanted my daughter's relationship with her father to continue even though ours was ending.

One day, there was a knock at the door. When I looked in the peephole, I noticed it was an uncle, my aunt's ex-husband. Before opening the door, I wondered why he was there. He never came to visit me before and we hardly ever spoke. I let him inside and we sat at the kitchen table talking.

He asked about the children first and then he asked where was my husband? I told him that I didn't know where he was, I hadn't heard from him and that we were no longer together. He sat quietly for a few minutes, then he closed his eyes and began nodding his head back and forth while humming. When he opened his eyes, he said, "Your husband is on his way back." I asked, "on his way back where?" He replied, "He's on his way back home." He told me to continue praying for him.

While those words sounded foolish coming from someone who hardly knew us, I welcomed the hope of reconciliation.

Meanwhile, I continued to raise our children to the best of my ability. I did not run the streets and I did not go out on any dates. Now, let's be very clear…it wasn't that I didn't want to, it was the fact that my relationship with God and living upright was of most importance to me. Not to mention, I was still married.

When my husband came to visit, there was no sign of reconciliation. I would go upstairs so that he could visit with his children. There was no visiting me because if he was interested in spending time with me, we would have still been together.

I recall a day he came over to visit and he wanted to be intimate with me. I kindly said no. I told him that we are not together, and I do not sleep around like that. It tickled me when he said, "But you're still my wife." I kindly declined again and told him the day he walked out that door, he walked out on our relationship and our relations. I said it and I meant it.

In the meantime, the kids and I continued going to church and I remember one Sunday, an older lady came up to me and said, “That’s not right Tanya, you need to let Steve see his daughter, you shouldn’t be keeping her away from him like that.”

I was heated, and I was about to let that woman have it in the worst way. Instead, I said to her “A lie doesn’t care who tells it.”

She continued, and I interrupted. Trying to respect my elders, I calmly told her that what she had heard was a lie and that I had never kept our daughter away from him. Then, I gathered my children and we left.

The more I thought about it, the angrier I became. I kept thinking I should’ve told her how Steve did not and would not give me any money for his daughter, but he went out and bought himself a Cadillac Escalade, which he parked right outside my window, so I would be sure to see it. He never came to pick her up and only visited three times… twice to see how I was surviving without him and the other time included him bringing an opened bag of pampers for our daughter.

The fact that Steve was going around lying on me, which he did often, really bothered me. Not only was he telling people that I wouldn’t allow him to see his daughter, but he was also telling people that I, not having any income whatsoever, put him out of his own duplex apartment. My name wasn't on anything in that apartment.

I was fed up. It did not appear that our relationship would be reconciled, so a few days later, I sought legal counsel. Then, I called Steve to have a conversation. I told him that I went to see an attorney about dissolving our marriage and that I filed for child support. I also told him that I did some research of my own and it was my understanding that we didn't have to wait a full year to be separated. I heard that we could go to the courthouse, agree that we've been apart for a year and do away with the marriage.

Somehow, things began to shift in our relationship for the better and we considered reconciliation. To reconcile, we had to first acknowledge and validate each other's feelings. As I have always said, "no matter how flat a pancake is, there are always two sides." Both of us played a part in our separation and it was going to take the both of us along with prayer, forgiveness, understanding and love to put our marriage back together.

During that time, one of my cousins said to me, "Tanya if I were you, I would still go through with the child support and have him pay you through the court just in case things don't work out, even if you have to give the money back to him."

I did not take her advice.

My belief is/was… a marriage cannot grow forward while sowing backwards. I trust in God and therefore a back-up plan is/was not needed.

We went to marriage counseling and we eventually reconciled.

I would encourage wives to apply one of my favorite scriptures, (NIV) 1 Peter 3:1, in your marriage. It says to be submissive to your own husband so that if he does not believe the word, that you may win him over not by discussion but by the way you live your life.

Let's look at the word "own." Why does scripture say, "your own husband?" I believe it is because some married women have major issues submitting to their "own" husbands but are more than willing to be submissive to another woman's husband.

Now, I'll address the part of that same scripture where it says, "that you may win him over not by discussion but by the way you live your life."

I had to stop trying to tell my husband what to do…easier said than done, right? It is not easy to keep quiet when you strongly feel that you know what is best in a situation. However, I have learned that all my talking did not win him over, my behavior is what won him over.

Another one of my favorite scriptures is Proverbs 18:22. It says "he who finds a wife, finds a good thing and obtains favor from the Lord."

Wives know that YOU are your husband's good thing; his gift, his treasure! You are the reason he obtains favor from the Lord.

Play your position in the marriage. Keep your mind on what you are doing to improve it. You have a choice to either use wisdom and build your home or be foolish and tear it down.

13

Now Faith

In July 2004, we purchased our first home. It was everything my husband and I had hoped for and wanted. About four months later, I arrived home with my daughters after picking them up from daycare. As I took off their coats and got them settled, I was rejoicing and singing praises to God for safely bringing my younger brother home from Iraq.

In the midst of my praise, my two year old daughter told me about the abuse that she and my other daughter were subjected to by the daycare provider's 40+ year old son. The daycare provider left her and my infant daughter in his care while she ran errands. Because of the abuse they experienced, I did not return to my job and subsequently resigned. Suddenly, we went from having two sources of income to one. I kept wondering what we were going to do and how it would work in our favor.

I was angry. I just could not wrap my head around my daughters being abused. I knew that I loved the Lord and I was called according to His purpose. I could not see it and I certainly could not understand it, but I knew that resigning from my job was somehow going to work for my good.

Well, my husband and I got to talking and I was telling him that I need to find a job where I can work from home. He suggested that I open a daycare. That sounded like a good idea, but I knew it would cost money to start a business and I didn't have any. I certainly didn't want to add more to my husband's plate as he was already doing so much.

I prayed and asked God to please help me and bless me that I will be able to open a daycare at home. I called to find out what I needed to do to get started and was told the first thing I needed to do was to attend orientation. When I called the number to register, I was told the class was full until February. I said to the woman on the other end of the line, "That's months from now, I cannot wait until February." I asked if there was another location and was told, "No, there is only one location for your county and that it is full until February."

I went on and asked her to go ahead and sign me up and she did. I sat at the table, talking to God, saying, "Lord, I'm just going to show up at the orientation next month. I'm not waiting until February." The only thing is, I didn't know the date of the next one.

I looked at the date on the calendar that she had given me for my orientation in February and it was the 3rd Wednesday of the month. I had an idea, so I called back. I asked for the date and time of orientation in March and it was a different date, but it was the 3rd Wednesday as well as the same time.

I hung up the phone and sat there thinking and talking to God again about how I was just going to show up, expecting to be admitted. I then said to myself, "Hold on…what's today?" I ran to look at the calendar. It happened to be the 3rd Wednesday. The clock was showing 23 minutes before the orientation was to begin, assuming there was actually an orientation that day.

I ran and gathered my things and scurried over to the location. The entire time, I was talking to God and telling Him how His

Word says that faith without works is dead. I said, "Now Lord, I'm going over here first expecting there is actually an orientation going on. Secondly, I'm going to get in!" I arrived at the location and there were a lot of people standing outside.

Excitedly, I was thinking that I'll just walk in and that be it. I thanked God all the way to the door. As I walked in, there were people sitting at tables, blocking the entryway, checking off names as they registered. I prayed, "Lord, I'm just going to walk right up, tell them my name, and let them know that I'm here for the orientation." That's just what I did. The woman checked her list, checked another list, and said, "Your name isn't on the list, but just sign right here and come on in." All I could say was Praise God!

14

Finances

Once I entered the room, I continued to give God thanks. The lady who sat beside me kept looking at me like I was crazy because I could hardly contain myself, smiling and mumbling praises to God under my breath.

During the orientation, I found out there was a lot of training that I needed to take to become a licensed childcare provider. The trainings, of course, cost money. The more I investigated the cost, the more I started to feel my momentum draining. Then, I said to myself, there's no way God is going to allow me to get here and not make a way for me to get the money I need for training to obtain my license. So, I started getting excited again.

The following Sunday we, my family and I, got dressed for church. Shortly before walking out the door, I remember saying, "Lord, if I just had $30, I would buy a family pack of chicken, some greens and some potatoes and Lord I would stretch that for two days." On our way to church, I started to cry a little and told Steve that I felt sorry about our current financial situation. I explained to him that I feel sort of responsible since I am the one who had to leave my job to take care of the children.

I then told him how I just wished I had $30 so I could make a better meal for all of us. He told me that it wasn't my fault and that it wouldn't be like that forever. We went to church and enjoyed the service. After the benediction, we chatted with friends for a few minutes and this beautiful woman walked over to me. She hugged me; put some money in my hand, balled my hand into a fist and said, "God bless you."

As she walked away, with tears in my eyes, I said, "God you are so good! Lord you care so much for me and I don't even know why you love me, but I'm sure glad you do!"

Now the thing that made it even more powerful is that I never told this woman my situation and as a matter of fact, I'd never talked to her. "Give, and it shall be given unto you; good measure, pressed down, and shaken together, and running over, shall men give into your bosom" is what God's Word says in Luke 6:38.

I started giving Steve "the eye" trying to tell him to wrap up the conversation he was having so that we could go because I was about to burst! I was smiling, thanking God, giving Him praise with my fist balled and all.

We finally left and as we were walking to the car, I reminded Steve about the $30 conversation I had with God and him before we left home. Then I told him what had just occurred with the nice lady putting something in my hand. He asked me what it was, and I told him it was some money. He asked me how much and I said, "I don't know, it was probably the $30 I asked God for earlier."

I was not opening my fist until I got into the car. I got in the car and opened my hand and it was $300! We sat there amazed at God's goodness for us. Now, not only did I have the money for food, but I had money to start my trainings for my childcare business. The same beautiful woman blessed me more times after that. She was God sent and I thanked God for her.

There were no words to express how grateful and thankful I was and still am for what she did for me. Because of her kindness, I was able to complete all my trainings, obtain my childcare license and open my business.

15

My Father

God blessed me with an amazing stepfather who I called my father. My father had integrity. His character was everything. I never had to wonder if he was being honest or not. He said exactly what he meant, and he meant what he said. His word was bond. My father was the best!

When I was young, we would play board games, cards and sometimes we'd go to the movies or roller skating at Anacostia Park.

My father spent quality time with us and was never too busy. He would come to the school to check on us. He made sure we were taken care of always and never let anyone take advantage of us.

As I got older, he would still take us roller skating, but he didn't skate because he was having pain in his hip area. I always thought the pain was in his legs because he walked with a limp.

Over the years, I had heard my father talking about having a hip replacement and he finally scheduled the surgery. He did not tell me the date; however, my mother knew the date and she didn't tell me either. They probably thought I would worry; they were right.

One day, I woke up around 4 a.m. from a bad dream. In my dream, it was on a Tuesday and I saw my father in a bed. He was not in the bed at the house he and my mother shared, but it was a different bed and he was dead. I woke up and cried hysterically as I fell onto the floor. My husband woke up to me crying loudly and asked what was wrong.

My first thought was to make up a lie because when I was younger, I was told if you had a bad dream and told it, it would come true, so I didn't immediately tell him. I tried to come up with something else to tell him. But really, nothing would explain the tears that I was shedding so I told him about the dream and said it was someone else. I cried, and I cried, and I couldn't stop crying. That dream seemed real!

I remember the day Mama called to tell me the date that my father was going to have a hip replacement. She was very nervous and didn't really want to talk about it.

The day before the surgery, while talking to my father on the telephone, he told me that he had a big bucket of fresh fish and he wanted to share it with one of his other daughters who asked if she could have some. It was late, and she had no transportation to their home and he was preparing for bed since he had to get up early the next morning. I then drove over to pick up the fish and dropped it off to her.

One of the reasons I did that is because I kept thinking about that dream. I knew if something happened to him that he had fulfilled the last thing he wanted to do for his daughter and their last memory would be a good one. The other reason is I believe in giving flowers while one can smell them, meaning I do what I can, while I can.

The following day, my father had a hip replacement surgery. I went to the hospital to visit him and he seemed to have been doing fine, recovering well. I told him he looked like he'd be getting out of the hospital soon and he agreed.

I went to the hospital every day, and every day, I hoped that my dream didn't come true.

My father started having pain in his stomach, unbeknownst to me. He asked my mother not to say anything because he didn't want us to worry. He ended up having an emergency surgery on his stomach and he started having a lot of pain afterward.

I was concerned about that because he went in for a hip replacement then needed surgery on his stomach…that didn't make sense to me.

I remember dropping off my mother to the hospital on a Monday as I ran errands. I got back to the hospital a couple of minutes after 8 p.m. and visiting hours were over. I remember pleading with the security guard at the desk to please let me go upstairs to see him and he told me that I could not. I told him that my mother was still up there, and I promised that I would only go and quickly speak to my father and leave, but he still would not let me in.

I had no other choice but to sit there and wait for my mother to come down. When I saw her, she looked very upset? She told me that he was in a lot of pain and that she had never seen him in pain like that before.

We had gotten half way home, and I turned around and headed back to the hospital so that my mother could tell the nurses some things that I thought it may have been, such as his bladder causing the pain in his stomach because he had not urinated in the hours that she was there visiting. She did, and we left the hospital again to head home. I dropped off my mother at home and I drove home.

My sister called me around 3 a.m. to tell me that my father had passed away. After hearing such devastating news, a calmness came over me. I sat on the edge of the bed, looked at the clock and thought, "Oh my gosh…today is Tuesday, it's after midnight…today is Tuesday!" I wept and then I began to give God praise. I praised Him for loving me enough to let me see this in advance. I felt if my father had passed away without warning, I may not have been any good. I probably would have lost it!

I thank God for my father. He meant the world to me. I watched him love, provide and protect my mother and our family. He always treated my mother with love and the utmost respect. He was a great example of what I expected from my husband.

I am also thankful to God that my father was able to walk me down the aisle on my wedding day. It was ten years before his passing.

16

Gun Play

When I was around nine years old, my big brother and I were outside playing, and we decided we would head home because darkness was approaching. We stood near the front steps of the apartment building where we had lived, talking to a few other people who also lived in the building.

One of them was an older boy and he was pumping some sort of rifle. He said he had been pumping it for the last two days and that he was going to use it to shoot a pellet at the stop sign across the street from where we were standing. Just as I turned to walk towards the door, a shot was fired, and my big brother yelled as if something had happened to him. We thought he was joking because he was too calm; not to mention, he had been standing near us the entire time. My big brother wasn't joking at all, however. The older boy accidentally shot my big brother in his back at close range.

I was scared. I started screaming and crying as I ran inside to get my mother. My big brother stayed calm; I'm thinking it was because he didn't want me to be worried. The paramedics came, and he was taken to the hospital. I'll never forget the doctor telling my mother that my big brother could have been paralyzed. I thank God for watching over him.

About eight years later, my big brother and I were at home and the doorbell rang. I looked in the peephole and I noticed it was a dude that hung out in the neighborhood. He was an associate of some of my family members. I opened the door and he put a 9-millimeter pistol to my forehead. I stood there in shock!

When my big brother walked into the room and saw what was going on, he yelled, “Man what are you doing?!” The dude started laughing and said he was “just playing.” As he lowered the gun he proceeded to tell us that the safety was on.

When I think about my big brother *accidentally* getting shot and almost paralyzed in comparison to someone who *intentionally* put a gun to my head and I didn’t get shot, all I can do is thank and praise God!

There are so many people who were killed because someone was “just playing” with a gun. I am so thankful that I was not one of them.

.

17

Armed and Dangerous

One thing I learned at an early age is that prayer changes things. Through prayer and meditation, God began to help me deal with people and my problems. I realized that He didn't bring me this far to leave me. Besides, in Deuteronomy 31:6, His Word says that He will never leave me, nor will He forsake me.

I would encourage you to arm yourself with God's Word. Read your Bible daily and establish a personal relationship with God, for He is our Father who art in heaven and He cares for us. If you do not understand your Bible, then pray and ask God for understanding. Proverbs 4:7 says, in all your getting, get understanding. There were times I would read my Bible and become frustrated. I first prayed about it and when I still didn't get it, I eventually purchased another Bible that I could better comprehend.

2 Timothy 2:15 tells us to study to show thyself approved. I don't know how many times I've heard people preach and/or quote phrases that are not in the Bible. I have found that some people will take lyrics from songs saying God said it and He has not, but you will not know unless you search the scriptures for yourself.

I would also like for you to know that God is not looking for you to be perfect or to seek Him when you "get yourself together." In Matthew 11:28, He said, "Come unto me all ye that labor and are heavy laden and I will give you rest," so all you need to do is come. In James 4:8, He also said draw nigh to

Him and He will draw nigh to you, just like that. He will meet you right where you are.

18

Study to Show Thyself Approved

I remember in the midst of all that was going on with my son's health, him being blind in both eyes, deaf in his left ear, experiencing severe pain crises, multiple hospitalizations, and him giving up on life, people had told me that God wouldn't put more on him than he could bear. I became angry after hearing that statement because God was our help! There was no way anyone could convince me that God is the one who put the sickness and disease on him.

Thinking more about the abuse I suffered, I remember having a conversation with a young lady about it and she said, "God won't put more on you than you can bear" and I told her, "I don't believe that God is putting sickness, disease and unimaginable pain on us and then telling us to either bear it or die. I just don't believe that." I remember asking where I might find the scripture to back up what was being told to me. The scripture I was given was 1 Corinthians 10:13.

That scripture was not new to me as I had read it many times and I have never understood it to mean that. I believe 1 Corinthians 10:13 means exactly what it says, "He will not tempt us beyond our ability to escape." This means that no matter how enticing a thing is, there is always a way to resist the temptation. This has absolutely nothing to do with God putting more pain on you than you can bear.

For instance, there have been people who have suffered the same complications of sickle cell disease that my son had and have died; he is still alive. Then there was the time I was pregnant and driving home when suddenly, a car crossed the center line and struck us head on. God kept me, my son and my unborn daughter. Again, people have died in that same instance.

God does not love us anymore than He loves you and in no way, did we survive because we could bear it.

I believe people are inadvertently taking God's Word out of context. If we are not careful, we can mislead people and cause them to become angry with God.

For this reason, I believe it is vital that we study to show thyself approved, read with understanding and develop a personal relationship with Him.

19

Be Made Whole

There are so many people suffering from things that have happened to them. In most cases, either something or someone has controlled their entire life. They can't move forward because they are still living in fear and a distrustful state of mind from past hurts.

Do not allow anyone or anything to steal another second of your life. I lived in bondage most of mines. I was alive but not living.

1 Peter 5:7 says that we should cast our cares upon Him because He cares. Matthew 11:30 says that His yoke is easy, and His burden is light.

I remember years ago, my best friend asked me to be in her wedding. It was an honor and I made myself believe that I could undress in front of her other bridesmaids until I had to face my reality. I looked in the mirror and didn't like all the scars that I had inflicted upon myself. The scars were not only shameful, but they were a constant reminder of the abuse.

I didn't want to talk about it and certainly didn't want anyone inquiring. At the last minute, I told her that I would not be a part of her big day and I felt horrible for letting her down.

God has since delivered me. I am no longer living in shame and I'm here to tell you that God can deliver you as well.

I encourage you to seek Him, pray to Him and make your request known unto Him.

Do not allow anything in your past or present to separate you from the love of God. I don't know why things happen the way that they do, but one thing I know is for certain: God wants you to have life and to have it more abundantly (John 10:10).

20

Timing is Everything

I have been praying for the right time to tell my son what happened to me. At first, it seemed like there was no right time to tell him, as he had been through so much with his health and in his life. A few months into 2016, I felt like it was time to tell him and I did. He was sad and said he was sorry to hear what I had gone through.

After I told him, I thought about a conversation my daughters had with me years ago, regarding my son. I will never forget the look on their faces as one of them said, "Awe, mommy, you had a baby and you weren't married?" I felt like I had really disappointed them.

However, after telling my son, I sat them down and told them what happened to me. First, I told them about my son's father and then I told them about my uncle. Without even mentioning my uncle's name, my daughters knew exactly which uncle it was. They said his name and I said yes, you're right!

When I asked them how they knew it was him, they told me they knew because he was the only uncle with which I didn't associate. They said, "You don't hug him, and you don't ever talk to him." At that moment, I realized how observant my children were.

Right when you think that they are not paying attention, they are watching and taking it all into perspective.

Months later, I saw my uncle at our family reunion and we spoke. I later explained to my daughters that I had forgiven my uncle for what he did to me, even though he didn't ask me for forgiveness. I also told them that I pray for him and that I hoped the best for him.

That night while I was praying, I thanked God for letting me finally get rid of all the baggage that was weighing me down for so many years!!

I felt like a huge weight had been lifted and it had!

21

Who Am I & What Do I Believe?

I am the daughter of My Father, Who art in heaven. I am flawed beyond measure; however, I try to live my life pleasing and acceptable to God.

When I trust in Him with all my heart and lean not to my own understanding, He directs my path. I know that the earth is My Father's and the fullness thereof. He will give me the desires of my heart. He will not withhold any good thing from me.

Galatians 6:9 says that I will reap if I faint not. Psalm 126:5 also says because I have sown in tears, I will reap in joy. Now, I am expecting my cup to run over with joy in every area of my life.

I am Happy, Healthy, Humble, Wealthy, Strong and Free.

Many are called but few are chosen, and God chose me.

He Kept Me.

Made in the USA
Middletown, DE
05 October 2018